More Than the ABCs

The Early Stages of Reading and Writing

Judith A. Schickedanz
Boston University

National Association for the Education of Young Children
Washington, D.C.

Book design: Cynthia Faber
Cover drawing: Nora, age 4

National Association for the Education of Young Children
1509 16th Street, N.W.
Washington, DC 20036-1426
The National Association for the Education of Young Children attempts through its publications program to provide a forum for discussion of major issues and ideas in our field. We hope to provoke thought and promote professional growth. The views expressed or implied are not necessarily those of the Association.

NAEYC wishes to thank the author, who donated much time and effort to develop this book as a contribution to our profession.
Library of Congress Catalog Card Number: 85-63122
ISBN Catalog Number: 0-912674-95-4
NAEYC #204

About the Author

Judith Schickedanz is an associate professor of Early Childhood Education at Boston University, where she teaches undergraduate and graduate courses in the teacher education program and serves as program coordinator. She has taught preschool and now serves as the director of The Early Childhood Learning Laboratory, a laboratory preschool in the School of Education at Boston University, where she conducts research on emergent literacy and continues to develop and test ideas that support literacy development in preschool children. She has authored texts on child development and teaching strategies and has written numerous articles on  early literacy development. Currently, she is helping to develop the curriculum for preschool programs as part of the Boston University/Chelsea Public School Partnership, an innovative university/public school collaborative.

To the letter **A**, for Adam.

Contents

Calendar   *106-108*

> Reading and writing, like other aspects of development, have long histories that reach back into infancy.

Chapter 1

Jumping Off the Page: Young Children's Written Language

If people on the street were asked what children learn in first grade, the most common answer surely would be that they learn to read and write. Most children do begin to read and write conventionally during the first grade. However, this accomplishment cannot be separated from children's earlier experiences that play a key role in learning and development.

Why is it important to think of learning to read and write as a process that begins years before first grade? We all know that before children walk, they sit up, crawl, and pull themselves up to stand. Before children use mature speech, they coo, babble, and use holophrases and telegraphic speech. Reading and writing, like these other aspects of development, have long histories that we now realize reach back into infancy.

Why does the idea that children's literacy development begins before children are instructed to read and write in the first grade seem so unbelievable? Let's look at some myths that can be dispelled by evidence gleaned from studies of children's literacy development.

Myth #1. Many people assume that oral language must develop before written language can begin (Mattingly, 1979). Because oral language itself is not mastered fully until about the age of 5, there are those who think written language development cannot possibly begin until after that time.

Evidence. Current research refutes this notion. Although oral language development certainly supports written language de-

Language develops best when adults include infants in conversation and when they treat them as conversational partners.

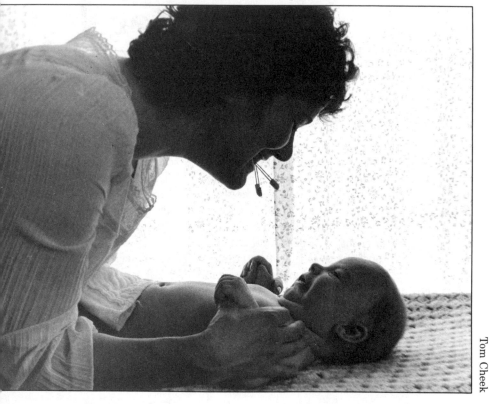

Tom Cheek

velopment, it does not appear to be a prerequisite in quite the way we previously believed. It appears that oral and written language develop simultaneously, with each area lending support to the child's understanding of the other (Ehri, 1975; Mason, 1980; Taylor, 1977).

Myth #2. People have also thought that oral language learning occurs naturally, while literacy learning must be tutored in specific ways. The conventional wisdom has been that very young children learn to talk just by being surrounded by talk, while being surrounded by print is not enough—children must be taught to read and write. Literacy learning, according to this way of thinking, does not start without the aid of formal lessons.

The tendency to think that written language learning is not a natural process has two major sources. First, the external circumstances that appear to support natural oral language learning have often gone unrecognized. Similarly, the natural beginnings of literacy development have been overlooked or dismissed as being unrelated to the conventional reading and writing behavior that appears later. As a result, we seem to have overestimated the extent to which oral language learning is natural (i.e., the result of simple unfolding no matter what the social circumstances), while we have underestimated the extent to which written language learning may occur in the absence of direct instruction.

Evidence. When we take a close look, oral language does not occur quite as naturally as was once thought. It occurs in a social context, not in a vacuum. If infants were placed in rooms with television sets, but without any live human beings, we might discover how unnatural oral language learning is. Infants learn to talk when meaningful talk is directed to them. Language develops best when adults include infants in conversation and when they treat them as conversational partners (Robbins, 1984; Wells, 1985).

Certainly children are predisposed to learning oral language. But it is misleading to claim that being surrounded by talk is enough. It is *being included in talk*, and *being treated like a competent language partner* that makes the difference.

When children are introduced to written language in a similar, socially mediated way, it appears that written language also occurs without the specific teaching we had assumed was necessary.

3

In instances where natural literacy learning has occurred, environments have been found to be rich both in physical resources and in social mediation (Bissex, 1980; Doake, 1979; Durkin, 1966; Forester, 1977; Red, 1975; Schickedanz & Sullivan, 1984; Schieffelin & Cochran-Smith, 1984; Teale, 1978; and Woodward, 1984). Teale (1982) explains the conditions which need to be met:

> In one respect there is a literacy environment "out there" from which children might abstract features of reading and writing. Considerable print exists in the preschooler's world, and virtually every child in literate societies like ours has the opportunity to observe others reading and writing. But . . . children who learn to read and write before going to school do not do so simply by observing others engaged in literacy events and by independently examining and manipulating a written language. In an important sense the child's literacy environment does not have an independent existence; it is constructed in the interactions between the child and those persons around him or her. . . . In fact, the whole process of natural literacy development hinges upon the experiences the child has in reading and writing activities which are mediated by literate adults, older siblings, or events in the child's everyday life. (p. 559)

Although we know relatively little about this aspect of parental behavior, it appears that parents vary considerably, both in the extent to which they mediate print for their children and in the specific ways they do it (Heath, 1983; Scollon & Scollon, 1981). The fact that more children master oral language without tutoring than is the case for written language may say more about differences between typical oral and written language environments than about differences in children's cognitive dispositions to learn one form of language versus the other.

It is also quite likely that much of children's early literacy development goes unrecognized. Ask parents when their child started to talk, and they will give the age at which the child *began* to use some well-articulated words, not the age when the child began to utter well-formed grammatical sentences. But ask parents or teachers when a child began to read or to write, and they are reluctant to give the child credit until behavior matches the conventional, or adult, model. Scribbling and retelling familiar story books tend to be discounted as merely pretend, not real, writing and reading.

Ask parents when their child started to talk, and they will give the age at which the child began *to use some well-articulated words. But ask when a child began to read or to write, and they are reluctant to give the child credit until behavior matches the adult model.*

We expect oral language to have a developmental history, beginning with immature, though bona fide, forms. Written language development, however, has not been viewed with a similar set of expectations, at least not until recently (Teale & Sulzby, 1986). As a result, we have often overlooked the literacy development that takes place early in children's lives.

Harste and his colleagues, who study what preschoolers know about written language, comment that elementary schools often fail to realize what preschoolers already know. "Many of the children who we came to perceive as 'very sophisticated 6-year-olds' were likely to be in formal reading and writing school programs which assumed they knew nothing about written language" (1981, p. 12).

First-grade teachers are not the only ones who fail to recognize young children's literacy knowledge and skills. Preschool teachers, too, often miss what happens right before their eyes, or they organize their programs so children have no chance to show them what they know.

In sorting through some old papers, I came across a yellow, crumpled piece of notebook paper. When I opened it, I found some scribble:

Underneath the scribble, the child's mother had written:

"Dear Miss Hoppin,
    Please do not get married. I want you to be the same old Miss Hoppin the way you are now.
                                        Love, Andrew"

Andrew was a 4-year-old in the preschool class I taught the year I got married. He wrote the note at home and brought it to me at school. I remember receiving the note from him and explaining that getting married would not change me in any significant way. But I do not remember Andrew's scribble writing or thinking about Andrew as a writer!

Now that I am no longer blinded by false assumptions about young children and literacy development, I don't know how I could have missed seeing Andrew as a writer. His knowledge about writing jumps off the page: He had organized his scribbles to appear print-like, not picture-like. His dictation took the form of a letter text, not the form of a story or a grocery list. If Andrew

---

Literacy learning proceeds naturally if the environment supports young children.

---

had suggested the idea of writing the note, then he also knew that thoughts can be saved for a later time when we write them down. And, since Andrew never spoke about his feelings before giving the note to me, he must have realized that some things are easier to bring up if they are presented first in writing.

I wonder now what else Andrew knew that simply passed me by. I am startled at the images that come back as I think about that classroom. Did I ever let the children show me what they knew about written language? The one pencil in the classroom hung by a string from the post of the easel so the *teachers* could write children's names on their artwork.

Our restricted views about what real literacy behavior includes, our faulty assumptions about how both oral and written language are learned, and our ignorance of the forms that early literacy behavior takes have led us to believe that the onset of literacy skills occurs more abruptly and much later than current research suggests. While most children may not read and write *conventionally* until they are 6 or 7 years of age (although some children do), many (probably most) children have considerable knowledge about literacy and are well on their way to becoming conventional readers and writers by the time they encounter their first formal lesson.

Fortunately, we now have much research to help us recognize literacy behavior in its early, nonconventional stages, and to help us understand that these early forms are important and necessary parts of the total stream of literacy development.

This book is intended to help teachers and parents understand literacy development in its early stages, and to learn how to support it. We begin at the beginning—with a discussion about babies and books. The book continues with discussions on how scribbling changes into script and how storybooks and other print experiences help preschoolers discover what reading is all about. This information about the course of literacy development is followed by suggestions for books and how to use them with children of various ages. In turn, you will find some ideas about how print and the tools to create it can be incorporated in a high quality environment for young children.

Throughout this book, we assume that literacy learning proceeds naturally if the environment supports young children. The goal for parents and teachers is not to teach children to read and write conventionally before they go to first grade, although many children who are provided with the kinds of opportunities to be described here always have, and always will, learn to do so. The goal is not to teach children to read and write at all, if by teaching we mean teacher-dominated instruction that consists of funneling bits of predigested information into children's heads.

The goal of this book is to help us make room for literacy learning, to give it a playful, interesting, useful, and joyous place in all children's lives, both at home and at school.

Bibliography

Atkins, C. (1984, November). Writing: Doing something constructive. *Young Children, 40*(1), 3–7.

Bissex, G. L. (1980). *GYNS AT WRK: A child learns to read and write.* Cambridge, MA: Harvard University Press.

Doake, D. (1979). *Preschool book handling knowledge or book experience and emergent reading behavior.* Paper presented at the annual meeting of the International Reading Association, Atlanta, GA.

Durkin, D. (1966). *Children who read early.* New York: Teachers College Press, Columbia University.

Ehri, L. (1975). Word consciousness in readers and prereaders. *Journal of Educational Psychology, 67,* 204–212.

Forester, A. (1977). What teachers can learn from "natural readers." *The Reading Teacher, 31*(2), 160–166.

Harste, J. C., Burke, C. L., & Woodward, V. (1981). *Children, their language, and world: Initial encounters with print.* Final Report of National Institute of Education Project # NIE-G-79-0132.

Heath, S. B. (1983). *Ways with words: Language, life, and work in communities and classrooms.* New York: Cambridge University Press.

Mason, J. M. (1980). When do children begin to read: An exploration of four year old children's letter and word reading competencies. *Research Reading Quarterly, 15*(2), 203–227.

Mattingly, I. Q. (1979). *Reading, linguistic awareness, and language acquistion.* Paper presented at the Reading Research Seminar on Linguistic Awareness and Learning to Read, Victoria, British Columbia.

Read, C. (1975). *Children's categorization of speech sounds in English.* Urbana, IL: National Council of Teachers of English.

Robbins, L. (1984, July). Mastering language: A process of give and take. *Bostonia, July,* 26–28.

Schickedanz, J. A., & Sullivan, M. (1984, January). Mom, what does u-f-f spell? *Language Arts, 61*(1), 7–17.

Schieffelin, B. M., & Cochran-Smith, M. (1984). Learning to read culturally: Literacy before schooling. In H. Goelman, A. Oberg, & F. Smith (Eds.), *Awakening to literacy* (pp. 3–23). Portsmouth, NH: Heinemann.

Scollon, R., & Scollon, B. K. (1981). *Narrative, literacy, and face in interethnic communication.* Norwood, NJ: Ablex.

Taylor, J. (1977). Making sense: The basic skill in reading. *Language Arts, 54*(6), 668–672.

Teale, W. H. (1978). Toward a theory of how children learn to read and write naturally. *Language Arts, 59*(6), 5455–5570.

Teale, W. H., & Sulzby, E. (Eds.). (1986). *Emergent literacy: Writing and reading.* Norwood, NJ: Ablex.

Weintraub, S., Smith, H. K., Moore, W. J., Jongsma, K. S., & Fisher, P. J. L. (Eds.). (1985). *Annual summary of investigations relating to reading: July 1, 1983 to June 30, 1984.* Newark, DE: International Reading Association.

Wells, G. (1985). *The meaning makers: Children learning language and using language to learn.* Portsmouth, NH: Heinemann.

Woodward, V. (1984). *Redefining literacy development: A social interactional perspective.* Paper presented at the annual conference of the International Reading Association, Atlanta, GA.

> Before you can suggest good books for babies, you need to know something about what the baby can do.

Chapter 2

Begin With Books

A boy sits on the floor looking at a book resting on his outstretched legs. He looks at a picture on one page, then carefully turns to the next. Slowly, he works his way through the entire book, then flips to the front to begin again. Unremarkable behavior, you might think, until you learn that the child is just 11 months old!

Although babies interact with books differently than older children do, even very young babies like books, and become engaged with them in significant ways. In this chapter we talk about babies and toddlers at various stages of their development, and about how they tend to interact with books. We also discuss how to organize a book nook in a group setting and what behaviors you can expect while reading to very young children.

Matching books to baby's development

Suppose you are browsing through the children's section in a bookstore when someone asks you to recommend some good books for a baby. Before answering, you would need to ask some questions. How old is the baby? Can the baby sit up? Can the baby grasp objects between the thumb and index finger? Does the baby recognize and name objects?

In short, before you could suggest some books, you need to know something about what the baby can do. A book that might be good for a baby in one stage of development may not be a good book for a baby in another stage of development. Let's look at some of the major characteristics of different ages and see how books can be matched with children's development.

Birth to 3 months

What babies can do. At birth, or soon after, newborns lying on their stomachs can raise their heads for brief periods. Gradually, they can lift their heads up for longer periods and can turn them easily from side to side. By 2 to 3 months most babies can lift their heads for quite a while when resting on their tummies, and they spend considerable time during waking periods looking around, especially if interesting objects are in front or to the side of them.

If held upright on a lap without support, a newborn's head will flop forward or to the side. Between 2 and 3 months of age, most babies become able to sit upright in a lap and maintain good head control.

Newborns can see objects clearly at a distance of about 10 inches from their faces. They like to look at patterns, instead of solid colors, and they prefer sharp contrast. For example, a bright or dark design on a white background is typically of more interest than is pale yellow on a pink background.

During the first months of life, babies cannot manipulate objects voluntarily, although they can grasp things reflexively if the objects are placed in their hands. By 3 months of age, many babies begin to bring things placed in their hands up to their mouths to suck.

Babies also produce sounds and respond attentively when others talk to them. At first, babies' typical sounds consist of crying and sucking, but certainly by 3 months many babies have added lots of coos to their vocalizing. They become especially vocal when they are in a good mood and someone smiles at and talks with them.

> # Recite rhymes or sing songs you know from your own childhood, since both book and baby cannot easily be held.

Books babies will enjoy. At this early stage, books will not play a dominant role in babies' lives. Eating, sleeping, diapering, and being held and cuddled will consume most of the day. However, a book can be something interesting to look at, and even babies this young will enjoy one or two.

Because infants are unable to manipulate a book, and because an adult needs to use both hands to support the baby's head, a shared book experience usually does not take place on a lap until babies can support their own heads well, at about 3 months old. Instead, open books flat and stand them at the side of the crib when a baby is resting on her or his back, or at the head of the crib when a baby is on her or his tummy. If the baby is placed on the floor for a short period, a book can be opened wide and placed at a comfortable viewing distance.

The ideal book for babies this age has simple, large pictures or designs set against a contrasting background, and is constructed so that it will stand up when opened. Stiff cardboard books, or soft but firm vinyl books, are usually good choices.

Paper pages, typical of preschool books, fall into the center of the book when the cover is opened wide enough to prop, which makes it impossible for babies to see the pictures. In addition, the illustrations often are too busy and lack the bold brightness and contrast that attract young babies' attention. Cloth books, too, are impossible to stand up, and often have illustrations that do not appeal to infants.

This early period is also a good time to introduce babies to the language of books. Nursery or other rhymes may be especially appropriate. Recite rhymes or sing songs you know from your own childhood, a helpful technique when both book and baby cannot easily be held. Young babies often settle down to the steady rhythm of these verses, which everyone appreciates!

Cloth and soft vinyl books are especially good for babies from 4 to 6 months.

4 to 6 months

What babies can do. During this period, babies usually become able to reach and grasp. Their grasp is more awkward than it will be later on, because the thumb does not yet resist the fingers. Instead, the grasp is a whole hand grasp. Virtually everything babies grasp is brought to the mouth for exploration. They also use their hands to bang on surfaces and to wave in the air.

Many babies learn to sit up by themselves around the age of 6 months or soon after. Sitting up frees their hands and sets the stage for them to use their newly developed reaching and grasping skills.

Cooing is well established by now, and babies and adults can engage in playful conversations. Babies experiment with sounds, and vocal play is common.

Books babies will enjoy. Looking without grasping is now a thing of the past. In fact, babies may look at a book very briefly during this stage. Instead, books will be chewed, sucked, shaken, and crumpled. A book is treated like any other object—as something to explore with the mouth and hands.

Cloth and soft vinyl books are especially good for this period because they are lightweight and compress in babies' hands as they are grasped. Thus, they are easier than a cardboard book to pick up. In addition, cloth and vinyl books do not disintegrate when they become wet, and wet they become after visiting so often a baby's mouth! Another advantage is that they can be washed, which is important if several babies share the same books.

Because babies can now hold their heads up, your hands are free to hold both the baby and the book. A baby sitting in your lap is apt to spend the most time looking at a book, rather than manipulating it. However, even in this situation, a baby is very likely to want to bat at the book or grab it between two hands to bring it to the mouth to chew or suck. Although you may wish to have several books with paper pages to share with the baby, it is a good idea to have a cloth or vinyl book close at hand in the event that chewing and mouthing seem to be the baby's preference.

It has been recommended that you place a toy in the baby's hand to decrease the infant's tendency to grab the book (Lamme & Packer, 1984). This might be tried and used if the baby seems content. I am not particularly bothered by the fact that babies like to chew on books, and suggest that babies simply be permitted to do so—if the books do not have paper pages that would be damaged, of course. Even here, I suggest that adults be willing, at least some of the time, to change the book, not the baby!

Simple, bright pictures set against a contrasting background are still the type of illustrations most likely to appeal to a baby at this age. Many cloth books do not have good illustrations, especially after they fade with repeated washings, so be careful to select those with especially appealing visual effects.

You will want to continue to recite or sing nursery and other rhymes to babies, and may want to read these from a book now, if a baby seems interested in looking while listening.

7 to 9 months

What babies can do. Babies of this age stay very busy—especially if they have many objects to explore. They continue to bang, wave, and shake objects, and begin to drop and toss them as well. Babies can transfer objects from hand to hand, which allows them to rotate and explore items more fully. Mouthing and chewing of objects continues, but these actions are frequently interrupted with episodes of visual inspection. When playing with an object, a baby is likely to bang, wave, chew, crumple, visually inspect, drop, retrieve, and then suck it.

Near the end of this period, babies can use their thumbs and index fingers to pick up small objects. This new skill is called a pincer grasp, and increases tremendously a baby's ability to handle objects. Babies can now point at things and skillfully stick a finger into or between things, such as the pages of a book.

Many babies begin to crawl by 7 or 8 months of age, and to pull to stand soon after that. Exploring objects with the hands while sitting may take a back seat for a while to the exhilaration of moving about.

Babbling, or syllable repetition, now enters the baby's verbal repertoire. Babies can say *"da-da-da-da-da"* and *"ma-ma-ma-ma-ma"* although these utterances will not have a specific meaning. Babies at this age also begin to comprehend even more of what others say.

Babies from 7 to 9 months can turn stiff, thick pages. Provide old magazines for babies to tear paper.

Michaelyn Straub

A major milestone of this period is the attainment of object permanence (knowing that even if an object is no longer in view, it still exists), although this ability is still quite fragile. If you playfully hide a ball under a blanket, for example, most babies will immediately lift the blanket and grab the ball. If an object is too difficult to find, however, babies will stop searching.

Books babies will enjoy. Babies' newly developed hand skills enable them to begin to try to turn pages of books late in this stage. Stiff, thick pages are easier for babies to turn than are pages made of cloth or vinyl, which are so soft that it is difficult to wedge a finger between the pages.

A special type of cardboard book, known as Chunky™, board, block, or Chubby™ books are especially easy for babies at this age to handle. These books typically are small, and are constructed so that the next page springs up when the previous page is turned, thus eliminating the need to separate pages that rest flat against each other.

Babies' ability to handle and explore objects, and their interest in seeing what objects will do, make paper especially intriguing now. Paper will be crumpled, torn, mouthed, and chewed. Obviously, books with paper pages cannot survive the independent play of babies of this age. Old magazines can be given to them so they can tear paper. If babies do not have a chance to explore and tear paper early, the pages of paper books may later become candidates for finding out about this interesting phenomenon. Keep babies from eating bits of paper, though—the chemicals used in color pictures may be harmful.

You will want to spend time holding a baby and reading books. Reading is most appropriate for children this young when you label pictures shown in books and read, what are by now, those familiar old nursery rhymes. Babies are not yet interested in stories, as such.

9 to 12 months

What babies can do. During this period, babies become much more skillful with their hands. By the end of their first year, many babies can place large pegs into holes, put rings on a post, and pull pop beads apart. These babies also are adept at eating finger foods such as dry cereal and bits of soft fruit or vegetables.

Learning to walk is a major achievement for many babies by this time. Their new mobility enables babies to get desired objects easily and to take them along while they wander about. You may find that infants now bring many objects to you. This is often the baby's way of saying, *"Play this with me."* When babies offer a book, they are probably using this action to say, *"Read this to me."*

Another major milestone near the end of babies' first year is the ability to say their first words, and to understand more and more of what others say. You can generally expect appropriate responses to questions such as *"Where is your nose?"* and to requests such as *"Give me a kiss."* Babies' improving certainty of object permanence combines with their increasing understanding of language so they may also respond appropriately to requests such as *"Go get the ball,"* or *"Let's find your shoes."*

The first glimmer of pretend play may emerge late in this stage, too. Babies may cuddle up with a favorite blanket, for example,

At about the age of 9 to 12 months a book's contents, rather than its physical characteristics, begin to capture more of children's attention.

and close their eyes, only to open them soon and smile and laugh. They seem to be saying, *"I was not really sleeping. I was only acting like I was."*

Babies at about 1 year of age are also beginning to make connections between objects and events. When you help them put on a jacket, they may say *"bye-bye"* or immediately head for the door. They will raise a comb or brush to their heads and move it back and forth.

Books babies will enjoy. It is at this time that a book's contents, rather than its physical characteristics, will begin to capture more of children's attention. Although babies still will explore a book physically, the contents will begin to dominate their interest. They now are beginning to recognize, understand, and relate objects and events in the world, and books which contain pictures of familiar things and activities are likely to be the ones babies will like best.

Chunky™ or Chubby™ books continue to be easy for children to manipulate because their pages turn easily, but they must be selected carefully in terms of content at this point. If the pictures are not of objects that are interesting to the baby, they may not have much appeal, even though their pages are easy to turn. Many babies are also skilled enough to manipulate the standard cardboard books with ease. There are many books of this kind to choose from.

Cloth books are still difficult for a baby to handle. If the book is permanently stiff, the pages are often thin and do not lay back flat once the page is turned. It is difficult for babies to keep the book open on a particular page. Limp cloth books have so much give that the entire book may be picked up when babies attempt to turn just one page. These books also fall in a heap as children attempt to sit with the book resting on their outstretched legs.

Books with paper pages still cannot survive babies' independent play. Although they tend to be more interested now in looking at pictures than in tearing pages, thin paper tears easily, and once a tear is made, the babies' attention may be drawn to this activity and away from looking at the book.

You may find that babies nearing their first birthday can talk quite a lot about the objects and events pictured in books, and that they will look as they listen. Some babies may even repeat

Because children are just beginning to sing from 12 to 18 months, they often enjoy books with songs.

sounds you make for objects such as trains, and they may try to repeat the names you give to the objects pictured.

12 to 18 months

What babies can do. Language usually begins to blossom during this period. Babies are able to say more words and to understand more, too. They like to name things, or point to things to request that they be named. Babies may also now use what is known as *expressive jargon.* The jabber is nonsense, but the intonation patterns resemble actual speech. By the end of this period, some children are beginning to combine two words to form primitive sentences.

Pretend play becomes more common and takes new forms: Objects are used for pretend activities, and dolls and stuffed animals may be taken for rides in wagons, or rocked to sleep, sometimes after a child reads them a story!

Television programs for children may be enjoyed now, and they may run to the set when a familiar theme song begins. Children may hum along with the familiar songs on these programs or with you as you sing songs to them. Objects, animals, people, and puppets may be recognized on the screen, and babies may begin sometime during this period to point to and name them.

Books babies will enjoy. Books with familiar content are still the type 1-year-olds enjoy the most. Because children are just beginning to sing, they often enjoy books with songs. Books with repetitious verses may also be favorites, and a 16- to 18-month-old may jabber along as the verses are read. This jabbering has been called *book babble*. Occasionally, a child may begin to fill in a few words in highly predictable and familiar books if you pause during the reading. Reading nursery rhymes encourages this activity, and some may be known very well indeed by now, if infants have been hearing them since soon after birth.

Actual stories may also begin to be of interest. The stories must be simple, of course, and should relate to events babies can easily understand from their experience. Theme books, which contain a series of related pages, with pictures and a few words, but not an actual plot, provide a good transition between the earlier point-and-say books (one or a few pictures on a textless page) which are used for naming things, and the simple, but bona fide, storybook, such as *Goodnight Moon*.

19 to 30 months

What toddlers can do. Language virtually explodes during this time period. The infant who uttered only a few words now becomes a toddler who talks in sentences. Toddlers' sentences typically are not well-formed grammatically (*"What you do?"* instead of *"What are you doing?"*; *"Two boy play."* instead of *"Two boys are playing."*), but they carry a lot of information, nevertheless, and one finds that an actual conversation is possible.

The child's interest in the world also expands rapidly. By the end of this period, the incessant *"Why?"* is often firmly entrenched in the child's verbal repertoire.

Pretend play continues to develop, too, and the child connects more and more individual actions into sequences. The older toddler might feed the doll, take it for a ride in the stroller, and then put it to bed.

Autonomy, both physical and psychological, emerges full force, although toddlers are also very dependent. One minute they can be sailing off on their own; the next minute, they might be holding on tightly to your leg.

By the end of this period, many children have graduated to a big bed, and have at least passing familiarity with a potty chair.

Books toddlers will enjoy. Actual stories really can be enjoyed now, and the many events of a toddler's busy life provide hints about what will be of interest. Stories about messy eaters, children who miss their mom and dad when they are away, and a child who bumps her head in a fall are sure to hit home. Stories about going to bed, sitting on a potty chair, and getting lost are also of interest.

Simple stories about how things work, or what makes things happen, will help to satisfy the toddler's urge to ask *"Why?"*, *"Why?"*, *"Why?"*, although every explanation may be met with yet another *Why*. It seems that the *Why* might be used as much as a way of keeping a conversation going, as a technique for obtaining information.

Illustrations can now be packed with information and action. Children will spend a lot of time looking at the pictures in a book, and asking questions about them. Books in which the pictures follow the text very closely will appeal to children, and they will attempt to relate what they hear you read with what the pictures show. Storybooks intended for children this age often have a picture on every page, accompanied by a small amount of text. The picture often shows exactly what the text says. This kind of book is ideal for the toddler. More complicated, and longer, stories do not illustrate every action, and these are intended for the older child. In addition, the active toddler's urge to get up and move will not endure a long story, particularly one read during the day.

Predictable books (pp. 66–70), that is, ones in which sentences are repetitive and rhyme, will delight the toddler, and will provide for the full participation and autonomy of action that toddlers often enjoy. In addition, their ability to sequence events, and to anticipate an event's place within a familiar sequence, makes simple predictable books very appealing to them.

Book behaviors

So far we have talked in general about babies' and toddlers' overall development and their book behavior. In this section, I will describe four specific types of behaviors you are likely to see when very young children interact with books: book handling, picture reading, story and book comprehension, and story reading.

This information has been gleaned from a number of sources describing studies of groups and individual children. Some were published long ago and others are more recent (Church, 1966; Hogan, 1898; Baghban, 1979; Butler, 1980; Leeds, 1983; Rhodes, 1979; Schickedanz, 1983).

Obviously, this is a very small sample of very young children on which to base definitive statements about their book behavior. But, it is all we have, so it is where we must start. Because of the extremely small number of children involved in these studies, **it is very important that you use these lists as** *guides* **to observe children's book behaviors, not as lists of expectations for what babies should do.** In fact, it would make sense to use the lists simply as a starting point for your own study of the book behavior of the infants and toddlers who are in your care!

The ages given indicate the range over which the behavior has been reported in these sources—they are clearly approximations. The behaviors are listed roughly in the order they appeared in the few babies that have been observed, but again I caution you to use this information as a guide.

Book handling

This group of behaviors deals with children's physical manipulation of books. These behaviors are the result of the interaction between characteristics of the book and characteristics of the baby. For example, a very young baby typically will maintain eye contact with the pictures in a book only if the pictures are simple, bright, and contain a high degree of contrast.

Children's book-handling behaviors you might observe are likely to develop in about this sequence.

1. Makes eye contact with the pictures, but without hand contact. (2–4 months)

2. Grasps the book with hands and brings it up to the mouth to suck and chew. Shakes, crumples, and waves the book. (5–10 months)

3. Deliberately tears paper pages, if offered. (5–15 months)

4. Helps an adult reader turn the pages. (7–8 months)

5. Gives the book to an adult to read. Hands the book back to the adult after one reading. Uses this action to request that the book be read again. (8–10 months)

6. Sits on an adult's lap or on the floor for extended periods (10 minutes or more) to look at books. Notable decrease in physical manipulation of books and increase in visual attention to books. (8–12 months)

7. Tears pages accidently due to difficulty in handling books, but stops tearing pages intentionally. (12–14 months)

8. Turns pages awkwardly. (8–12 months)

9. Turns pages well. (11–15 months)

10. Flips through a book by gathering a clump of pages in a hand and letting them fly past. (14–15 months)

11. Turns an inverted book right-side up, or turns head as if trying to see the picture right-side up. (11–15 months)

12. May continue to rotate a book in an attempt to get a picture right-side up if something in a picture is actually upside-down. For example, if a clown is standing on her head on one page of the book and all objects are upright on the facing page, one rotation rights one picture, but inverts the other. The next rotation reverses the situation, and so on. The child continues to rotate the book, apparently in an attempt to get everything right-side up. Because an inversion problem of this kind cannot be solved, the child may become frustrated and lose interest. (16–20 months)

13. Recognizes the difference between a book that is oriented incorrectly (is upside down) and one in which a picture on a particular page shows something that is *intended* to be upside down (such as a sloth hanging from a branch of a tree). Does not rotate the book, or at least soon stops doing it and does not become frustrated. (24 months)

Picture reading

This group of behaviors describes ways in which children may interact with the pictures in books.

1. Intensely looks at pictures. (2–4 months)
2. After hand and mouth manipulation have subsided somewhat, returns to intensely looking at pictures. (8–10 months)
3. Laughs or smiles at a familiar picture, usually one for which the adult makes an interesting sound, or reads about in an unusual way. (8–12 months)
4. Points to individual pictures. (8–12 months)
5. Vocalizes (usually unintelligibly) while pointing to a picture. (10–12 months)
6. Points correctly to a familiar object pictured when asked, *"Where's . . .?"* (11–14 months)
7. Names objects pictured. (10–14 months)
8. Makes animal or other sounds (choo-choo) when the appropriate, familiar pictures are seen in books. (10–13 months)
9. Points to pictures and asks *"What's that?"* or indicates in another way (*"Dat?"* or questioning intonation) that a label is desired. (13–20 months)

Story and book comprehension

Babies and toddlers can demonstrate in a variety of ways that they understand what a book is about or how something shown or said in a book relates to another book or to events and objects in their own experiences. Some of those ways are listed here.

1. Laughs or smiles at a picture, as if to indicate recognition. (8–12 months)
2. Relates an object or an action in a book to the real world (e.g., goes to get a teddy bear after seeing a picture of one in a book). (10–14 months)
3. Selects books on the basis of their content, thus demonstrating understanding of what a book is about (e.g., picks up a book with a picture of a duck in it after playing with a toy duck). (10–15 months)
4. Shows a favorite page of a book by searching for it or holding the book open at a certain page repeatedly, as if the part is particularly well understood or appreciated. (11–14 months)

5. Performs an action that is shown or mentioned in a book (e.g., wants to feed the kitten milk after reading about it). (12–23 months)

6. Makes associations across books (e.g., retrieves a second book about ducks after reading one about ducks, or gets two books and shows that they contain similar pictures, events, etc.). (20 months)

7. Shows empathy for characters or situations depicted in books (e.g., pretends to cry after being told that a child shown in a book is sad). (16–20 months)

8. Talks about the characters and events in storybooks in ways which suggest that what has been said or read has been understood. Relates events in books to own experiences. (20–26 months)

Story reading

These behaviors refer to children's verbalizations in interaction with the connected text (rhymes or actual stories) in books, and with the child's dawning awareness that the words said when reading a book are printed in the book.

1. Uses book babble. (The child jabbers while looking at a book. Book babble sounds like reading rather than conversation, although what is said is nonsense.) (13–14 months)

2. Fills in the next word in the text when the adult pauses, says the next word before the adult reads it, or reads along with the adult. (15–28 months)

3. Reads to dolls or stuffed animals. (17–25 months)

4. Indicates that print in books is noticed (e.g., points to labels under pictures as the pictures are named). (15–20 months)

5. Says part of the text on a page immediately after the page has been turned. Knows what the page says by seeing the illustrations. (Note: What is said may just be one word of text, such as when a child says *"Hush"* while being read *Goodnight Moon.*) (17 months)

6. Recites text from a story outside of the story-reading context, for example, when swinging in a swing. (21 months)

7. Recites whole phrases from favorite stories, if adult pauses. (24–30 months)

8. Asks to read books to the adult, and may be able to recite several books fairly accurately, especially if they are predictable (see Chapter 3, pp. 66–70) or familiar books. (28–34 months)

9. Protests when an adult misreads a word in a familiar, and usually predictable, story. Typically offers the correction, too. (25–27 months)

10. Moves finger or whole hand across a line of print and says what it says. The rendition may be the exact text or an accurate paraphrase. (32 months)

11. Reads familiar books to self and provides very accurate renditions of the text, particularly if the books are predictable. (30–36 months)

Summary of early book behaviors

Very young children differ considerably in all aspects of behavior, and book behavior is no exception. Some babies between the ages of 5 and 10 or 12 months literally devour books, while other babies are content to look at books without taking them in hand . . . and mouth. Some babies enjoy sitting in a lap and being read to, as if they simply enjoy listening and looking, while other babies struggle down from laps and stop by only for brief episodes of book reading. Some babies settle down to sleep with gentle rocking and nursery rhymes, while others fight sleep in general and would be stimulated too much, particularly in the early months, if adults recited nursery rhymes or sang songs.

How a specific baby interacts with a specific book at a specific time will depend on that baby's style of interacting with the world in general, the baby's past book-playing and book-reading experiences, the characteristics of the book at hand, and the baby's general level of development in such areas as motor and language skills. Most babies probably will exhibit behaviors similar to the ones listed earlier, although each baby will do so in her or his own good time and way.

As a sensitive parent or teacher, you will watch the baby and try to adjust experiences and interactions to match what the baby can, and likes to, do. In short, we must read the baby, if we are to be effective in reading *to* the baby.

Create a book nook

If you are responsible for babies in a group setting such as a child care center, family day care home, or play group, you will need to consider how to make books available to them.

> A good arrangement for a book nook for babies is to stand some books up on the floor while others are simply laid down flat.

Babies younger than 4 months of age will need books in their cribs or nearby on the floor to look at when they are placed on their stomachs. It is a good idea to set some books aside especially for these younger babies.

Babies between 4 and 7 or 8 months are usually not yet mobile, so books will also need to be taken to them. Because children of this age so often put books in their mouths, it may be best to set another group of books aside especially for their use. These books can then be washed at frequent intervals.

Older babies will enjoy a special book nook. Crawlers and walkers can get to an area where books are attractively arranged and easy to reach. The typical, upright book display racks so popular in preschool classrooms are not very functional in an infant room. Babies are not tall enough to reach the higher shelves, and unseasoned crawlers and walkers can topple if they must reach to obtain materials.

A good arrangement for a book nook is to stand some books up on the floor while others are simply laid down flat in the same area. The standing books can be seen from a distance and will catch the children's attention. A corner of the room will serve best because traffic will not go through the area. Make sure the area is covered with carpeting or a rug so sitting will be comfortable.

Pillows are not necessary, nor are they a very good idea. Babies often don't watch the floor when they walk, and they can trip over pillows. In addition, a book is easiest for a baby to handle in the lap, while sitting. Leaning against a pillow puts a baby in a position that makes manipulating a book difficult.

Just because you provide a special place in the room for books does not mean that books must stay there. Babies will get a book, perhaps look at it for a short while, and then carry it with them as they go to another area of the room. They might set the book aside while they engage in another activity, and then pick the book up again. Babies might be encouraged gently, and helped, to return books to the book nook when they truly are finished with them, but remember that a baby does many things while on the run. Limiting book use to the book area will seriously limit babies' book interactions, and this seems unnecessary and unwise.

A book nook can be thought of, not so much as the only place where books belong in the room during play, as the place where babies can go to find a book if they wish to have one. It is also an out-of-the-way place where adults know they can read to children without being in the way of other activities.

How to read to a baby

Be sensitive to children's signals

Many of us are accustomed to thinking of our experiences with preschoolers when we think about reading to children. A storybook comes to mind, and we think of a group of four to six children gathered around us, listening intently as we read. Children may ask questions: *"What's Max doing with those monsters?"* Or they may relate the story to their own lives: *"The fire engine came to our house one time."* Preschool children also verbalize their feelings and desires: *"I don't like that book. Read this one instead,"* or *"Read that one again!"* Reading to a baby, however, is a very different undertaking.

First, as mentioned earlier, babies do not appreciate actual stories until they are well into their second year. Books for babies contain pictures with no story text. These books are to look at and talk about, and this is much of what reading to a baby is all about. But a baby's attention even to these activities is often fleeting and unpredictable.

There are times when infants simply like to manipulate books with their hands, or chew or suck on them. If we try to hold a book away from a baby's mouth so that pictures can be seen and talked about, we may become frustrated when the baby grabs the book back again. But babies of 6 or 7 months surely will do just that. We must learn to appreciate infants' ways of interacting with books. Later on, they probably will enjoy looking at the book instead of chewing on it.

It may seem to adults who read to walking infants that they cannot make up their minds whether they want to look at a book or not. A baby may sit on your lap for a minute or two, get up to do something else, and then return to you for a few more minutes with renewed interest in the book. This time, the baby may sit for a few more minutes and then go off again.

While some children between 12 and 18 months sit quietly on a lap for extended periods of time and look at books, many infants enjoy books only for a few brief minutes at a time, and return for several such episodes over a period of time. Babies between 12 and 18 months usually attend to books the longest during reading times that precede bedtime, both during the day and at night. The baby is tired then, so is less active, and enjoys the holding and talking that accompany looking at books.

One reason why babies may be so physically active during book reading is because physical movement is the way they express excitement or thoughts the book elicits. For example, when he was around 12 months of age, my son Adam became very excited when he saw a picture of a duck in a book. He was crazy about ducks around this time, perhaps because of our many trips to a duck pond near our home. Often he jumped out of our laps and ran to find his rubber duck, a constant bathtime companion. Or, he walked through the house saying, *"duck, duck, duck,"* in a tone that suggested great excitement. Often he returned to our laps to resume looking at the book, unless he had found something else to do during his wanderings.

Older children might be able to express their excitement verbally. *"That duck in the book looks like the duck I play with in the bathtub!"* Older children make the journeys in their minds, while babies must make the actual journey. In addition, older children are no longer surprised or delighted in the same way as younger children who have not yet become accustomed to expecting books to contain pictures of things in their own world. A baby who is just finding that familiar objects show up in books is overjoyed with each discovery, and the excitement is often expressed through physical activity.

It requires special understanding, patience, and sensitivity to play with babies and books. If we can learn to respond to babies' signals and to share books with them on their own terms, books can be the basis for many happy moments for all of us.

There are times when infants simply like to manipulate books with their hands, or chew or suck on them. Later on, they probably will enjoy looking at the book.

Story-reading strategies

When we read to children during their first year or two, we seem to follow a particular language format. First, we get the baby's attention, or focus the baby's attention on a picture in the book. By saying *"Look!"* or *"Oh, look at that!"* we get the baby to orient toward a picture in a book. Then we ask a question. *"What's that?"* or *"What does that do?"* or *"What do you see there?"* are examples of such questions.

At this point, the baby may vocalize in some way, smile as if the picture is recognized, or stare blankly at us, as if she or he hasn't the foggiest notion about what the object is. In any event, the baby or the adult provides an answer to the question, which in this case consists of a label for the picture being discussed. If the baby anwers with a smile or a gurgle, or even with a word, we typically say something like *"Yes,"* and then give the answer or repeat the child's answer in a well-articulated form (*"Yes, that's a monkey, isn't it?"*) If the baby answers, but mislabels the picture, we might say, *"Well, it is brown like a dog, but that's a monkey. Monkeys have l-o-n-g tails."*

In short, the format used in story reading to babies of this age seems to follow a four-part sequence:

1. get the baby's attention,
2. ask the baby a labeling question,
3. wait for the baby to answer, or if necessary, provide the answer yourself, and
4. provide feedback (Ninio & Bruner, 1978).

The adult literally carries the dialogue forward in these episodes, because the baby's productive language is limited. Ninio and Bruner refer to the adult's behavior as *scaffolding*, which means that we provide the overall language framework and fill in most of the slots in the dialogue. As infants grow older, they are able to participate more and more, and we allow them to take the lead.

We know relatively little about adult-child language during story reading, both during this very early period, and later during the preschool years. Ninio and Bruner's study was intensive, but involved only one mother-child pair. However, it does appear that adults vary in the way they share books with children.

For example, some adults relate the text to the child's own experiences and ask factual questions about the story after the book has been read, but other adults do not. We do know that

> being read to is not the seamless whole that it has been considered in much previous research. . . . Therefore, we should not be content merely to find out how much a child has been read to . . . and then relate the amount, or the presence or absence, of this type of experience to literacy development. We also need to attend carefully to the nature of the activity itself. (Teale, 1984, p. 113)

You might find it interesting to tape-record some of your book-reading sessions with individual infants. One session could be recorded every couple of months for a 6- or 8-month period. Then the three or four episodes obtained could be listened to and discussed in terms of how the baby's participation has changed, and how the adult's reading strategies also have changed. Tapes of this kind provide wonderful material for staff meetings and staff-training sessions.

Your observations and insights about babies and books could be valuable in building a much broader information base than we now have about how we can appropriately use books with very young children.

References

Baghban, M. J. M. (1979). *Language development and initial encounters with written language: A case study in preschool reading and writing.* Unpublished doctoral dissertation, Indiana University, Bloomington, IN.

Butler, D. (1980). *Cushla and her books.* Boston: Horn Book.

Church, J. (1966). *Three babies*. New York: Vintage.

Hogan, L. E. (1898). *A study of a child*. New York: Harper & Brothers.

Lamme, L., & Packer, A. (1984). *Reading with infants*. Paper presented at the annual conference of the International Reading Association, Atlanta, GA.

Leeds, S. (1983). *A mother's diary*. Unpublished mimeo paper.

Ninio, A., & Bruner, J. (1978). The achievement and antecedents of labeling. *Journal of Child Language, 5*, 1–15.

Rhodes, L. (1979). *Visible language learning: A case study*. Urbana, IL: ERIC/EECE. (ERIC Document Reproduction Service No. 199 653)

Schickedanz, J. A. (1983). *Literacy begins in babyhood: Notes from a mother's diary*. Unpublished mimeo paper.

Teale, W. H. (1984). Reading to young children: Its significance for literacy development. In H. Goelman, A. Oberg, & F. Smith (Eds.), *Awakening to literacy*. Portsmouth, NH: Heinemann.

Suggested books for babies

Books for the very young baby to look at

Bruna, D. (1980). *My Toys*. Los Angeles: Price, Stern, & Sloan. This is a zig-zag rather than a bound book, which makes it easy to prop. The pictures are simple and the colors used are bright and full of contrast. (A number of zig-zag books are on the market. These are good for propping up, but be sure to inspect the illustrations carefully. Several have detailed illustrations that are in pastels, not illustrations that are simple, bright, and full of contrast.)

Johnson & Johnson's *Visual Display*. Skillman, NJ: Johnson & Johnson. This book toy is constructed especially for propping. It consists of two separate panels with three sections (pages) each. The sections can be folded and interlocked to form triangles, which stand up especially well. The pictures and designs are simple, bright, and contain ideal contrast to catch the attention of a young baby.

Books of nursery rhymes and songs (appropriate for the younger and older infant alike)

Aliki. (1968). *Hush little baby: A folk lullaby*. Englewood Cliffs, NJ: Prentice-Hall.

Chorao, K. (1977). *The baby's lap book*. New York: Dutton.

Rackham, A., illustrator. (1975). *Mother Goose*. New York: Viking.

How to read stories to babies

1. Get the baby's attention. (*"Oh, look!"*)
2. Ask the baby a labeling question. (*"What's that?"*)
3. Wait for the baby to answer, or if necessary, provide or elaborate upon the answer. (*"Yes, that's a monkey, isn't it?"*)
4. Provide feedback. (*"Well, it is brown like a dog, but that's a monkey. Monkeys have l-o-n-g tails."*)

Rosetti, C. (1968). *Sing song: A nursery rhyme book.* New York: Macmillan.

Most children's bookstores and libraries have a number of good volumes of rhymes and songs. Look for one that meets your needs and that you like.

Books that can stand a young baby's manipulation
(cardboard, cloth, and soft vinyl books)

Dick Bruna Cloth Book Set. (1976). *Dressing, Working,* and *Counting.* Toys To Grow On, P.O. Box 17, Long Beach, CA 90801. Cloth books with simple, vibrant illustrations.

Greeley, V. (1984). *Zoo animals, pets, and field animals.* New York: Harper & Row. Cardboard, with beautiful illustrations.

Looking at animals. (1981). Los Angeles: Price, Stern & Sloan. Very colorful and made of stiff cardboard.

Miller, J. P. (1979). *The cow says moo.* New York: Random House. A cloth book with fairly good illustrations.

My house, My yard, and others. (1978). New York: Golden Press. Cardboard, bright illustrations, and relatively small.

Books with pages that are easy to turn (especially nice for babies who are just beginning to turn pages)

Baby animals. (1983). New York: Macmillan. A block book with cardboard pages.

Mother Goose rhymes. (1984). New York: Simon & Schuster. This is a super Chubby™ book with cardboard pages.

Sesame Street. *Ernie and Bert can . . . can you?* (1982). New York: Random House. This is a Chubby℠ book with cardboard pages.

Smallon, M. J. (1981). *The alligators ABC*. New York: Random House. This is a Chunky℠ book with cardboard pages.

Phillips, M. (1984). *Cats to count*. New York: Random House. This is a Chunky℠ book with cardboard pages.

Books that are good for naming things (especially appropriate for the baby between 9 and 18 months of age)

Baby's first book. (1960). New York: Platt & Munk. Cardboard pages with several pictures to a page.

Bruna, D. (1967). *B is for bear*. Los Angeles: Price, Stern & Sloan. Paper pages, so not for independent play.

Gillham, B. (1982). *The first words picture book*. New York: Coward, McCann, & Geoghegan. A colorful book of photographs of common things. Paper pages, so not for independent play.

Looking at animals and *Going for a ride*. (1980). Los Angeles: Price, Stern & Sloan. Colorful, short, cardboard books with one picture to a page.

McNaught, H. (1976). *Animal babies*. New York: Random House. Paper pages, so not for independent play.

My first look at clothes. (1991). New York: Random House.

Scarry, R. (1985). *Best word book ever*. New York: Golden Press. Paper pages with many pictures to the page. Not for the child under 1 year of age, but loved by many over that age. Provides many hours of pleasure for the child who likes to name things . . . or have them named.

Books with simple stories (babies who are just beginning to be able to sit long enough to listen to a real story)

Brown, M. W. (1947). *Goodnight moon*. New York: Harper & Row. Lots of repetition and easy to understand. A good story to read at bedtime.

Burningham, J. (1975). *The blanket*. New York: Crowell. A very short story about an object most dear to babies' hearts.

Carle, E. (1972). *The very hungry caterpillar*. New York: Philomel. Repetitious text involving many familiar foods and a caterpillar.

Fujikawa, G. (1957). *Faraway friends*. New York: Grosset & Dunlap. Cardboard pages. This is more a theme book than an actual story—content is related from page to page.

Fujikawa, G. (1957). *Here I am*. New York: Grosset & Dunlap. Another cardboard theme book. Nice pictures and some familiar things to talk about.

Fujikawa, G. (1975). *Sleepytime.* New York: Grosset & Dunlap. Another cardboard theme book. More nice illustrations and things to talk about.

Krauss, R. (1945). *The carrot seed.* New York: Harper & Row. Paper pages and very simple text.

> Experience with books during the preschool years is related to successful literacy development during the elementary school years.

Chapter 3

Preschoolers and Storybooks

Experienced teachers and parents know that young children are sticklers when it comes to making sure that familiar books are read exactly as they are written. Miss or change a word, and you are likely to be corrected. But is this behavior important?

Recent research and theory indicate that such behavior may be a fundamental milestone in literacy development. In this chapter, we discuss the story-reading behavior typical of the preschool period, what story-reading experiences are thought to contribute to overall literacy development, and how parents and teachers can facilitate this development.

From story reading to literacy

Children who learn to read naturally before entering school usually also have extensive story-reading experience (Doake, 1981; Durkin, 1966; Clark, 1976; Plessas & Oakes, 1964; Sutton, 1964). Similarly, researchers have found that experience with books dur-

Young children are sticklers when it comes to making sure that familiar books are read exactly as they are written. Such behavior may be a fundamental milestone in literacy development.

ing the preschool years is related to successful literacy development during the elementary school years (Wells, 1981). This strong correlation between early story reading and later literacy success has led many to conclude that there is a direct link between the two. For example, as children first become acquainted with books as infants, toddlers, and preschoolers, they learn

1. how books work,
2. print should make sense,
3. print and speech are related in a specific way,

> # Children who learn to read naturally before entering school usually also have extensive story-reading experience.

4. book language differs from speech, and
5. books are enjoyable.

In addition, if books are read to children in certain ways, and if the conversation surrounding the book-reading experience has certain characteristics, children may learn

6. patterns of interacting characteristic of behaviors expected in a school setting.

Learning how books work

Part of knowing how to read involves knowing some basic conventions about books and print. For example, books begin and end in certain places, and they are scanned in a certain direction. Books printed in English are read from front to back, left to right, and top to bottom. While this knowledge seems reasonably simple and straightforward, we probably should not overlook the comfort that accompanies total familiarity with such access procedures.

We all feel more comfortable when we are certain we know what to do with an object and have figured out how it works, especially when we are in an environment where that object is all-important (i.e., books in school). Conversely, being aware that you do not know the purpose or way in which something works is at least a little disconcerting. It's probably somewhat like the feeling many of us adults have today about computers. We do not feel comfortable with them at first, and we may avoid even coming in contact with them. It really can be a struggle, both physically and emotionally, to get the hang of something new, especially when you feel you must because an important aspect of your life depends on it. Children who literally grow up with books never face this struggle in learning to read.

Michaelyn Straub

It really can be a struggle, both physically and emotionally, to get the hang of something new, especially when you feel you must because an important aspect of your life depends on it. Children who literally grow up with books never face this struggle in learning to read.

Learning that print makes sense

One of the fundamental insights we need if we are to learn to read is that print makes sense (Smith, 1983; Goodman & Goodman, 1980; Holdaway, 1979). Words are not strung together at random to form nonsense phrases. They are placed together in a meaningful way. Although good readers rarely think about it, we

If we expect print to make sense, we can predict the text as we read along and monitor our decisions about what words are there. This expectation is a powerful device in helping us read.

constantly monitor whether the text makes sense. If something does not make sense, we quickly retrace our steps and change a word we previously read so that it does fit in terms of meaning.

If we expect print to make sense, we can predict the text as we read along and monitor our decisions about what words are there. Of course, we look at print to know precisely what word is there, but the possibilities are narrowed considerably by what we know would make sense. This expectation is a powerful device in helping us read, and it is one that the poorest readers often lack.

Some children sound out words and move on from one word to the next even if the word they pronounce fails to coincide with one they have in their oral vocabulary, or one that makes sense in the context of the text. When they finish reading in this way, many very poor readers say they do not know what the text was about. But they plowed through it anyway, as if the object of reading was to say or call out the words, rather than to derive meaning.

But how do other children acquire the expectation that print should make sense? Surely one source must be experience with storybooks. In hearing stories, the first and most abiding focus is on the meaning. Children's attention is not directed toward individual letters or words; it is on what the story is about. When storybooks are included as a major part of a child's introduction to the printed word, the expectation that print should make sense is communicated from the start.

Along with experience with books is another critical factor that helps children make sense from print. When children have a broad knowledge about the world, when they have a variety of experiences with people, places, and things, the chances are greater that text will be meaningful, because the ideas and concepts are familiar to them.

Experience with books, and experience in general, both help assure that words make sense to young children.

Learning that print and speech are related

Suppose we found ourselves in the midst of a society that had no written language, and we were asked to create it. First, we would need to make a very basic decision: At what level would our writing system represent speech? Would we create a *logo-*

> When children have a variety of experiences with people, places, and things, the chances are greater that text will be meaningful, because the ideas and concepts are familiar.

graphy (i.e., an orthography or writing system that represents speech at the word level), a *syllabary* (i.e., an orthography that represents speech at the syllable level), or an *alphabetic orthography* (i.e., a writing system that represents speech at the phonemic level)? Each system is used today. For example, the orthography used to represent Chinese is a logography, while the orthography used to represent Japanese is syllabary. English is represented by an alphabetic orthography.

Each system has its advantages and disadvantages. The units of speech represented by logographies and syllabaries may be easier for us to segment in speech, but they require us to learn a large number of unique symbols. For example, there are about 70,000 characters used to write in Chinese (Taylor, 1981).

A syllabary needs far fewer symbols than a logography, because the same syllable appears in many different words, but the number is still large compared with the number of unique symbols used in alphabetic orthographies. For example, we must learn only 26 unique letters to be able to write any English word. There is, however, a disadvantage to the admittedly efficient alphabetic orthography: The level of representation does not match the level of speech that seems to be the most meaningful and easiest to isolate (Liberman et al., 1974).

Menyuk (1976) has suggested that in "real speech processing" the focus is on words and on relations between words, because this is where meaning is to be found. Conscious phonemic analysis is not required to any great extent in oral language processing, and children are not accustomed to thinking about speech at this level. In addition, many phonemic elements, as we have come to think of them for the purpose of representing each with an alphabet letter, do not exist in pure form in the stream of real speech. Although we learn *to think about* words in terms of individual sounds, any demarcation between these is blurred in actual speech. Even when we try to sound words out, it is difficult to emit one sound in isolation.

Young children are not yet at the stage where they can deal with something that is this abstract. We cannot hold onto speech and manipulate it the way we can other objects, and yet, in a sense, this is exactly what children need to do as they develop their language skills. Furthermore, speech manipulation needs to take place in the context of print, if children are to gain the necessary insight, because it is the *relationship* between speech and print that is the puzzle.

Storybooks may play an important role in the development of this insight because they put children in a position to hold onto and manipulate speech in relation to print and to discover how they are related (Mason, 1980; Schickedanz, 1978). The simple and predictable text found in many picture books, along with the repeated readings that typically accompany the picture book experience, often lead children to learn the lines of several stories by heart. Young children often know the text exactly, and on which page the various parts of the text belong. This oral knowledge of the text provides a powerful monitoring device when children become interested in figuring out how the print they see on each page actually "works" to represent the story they know how to say.

At first, children may assume that each letter in print represents a spoken word, or a syllable, rather than a sound. But if a child acts on the basis of this assumption, she or he ends up with print left over when the oral rendering of the text has been completed. For example, here is what will happen:

Once upon a time,   (text)

Once upon a time,   (child's verbalization with fingerpointing—child points to *each letter once* for every word spoken)

Because the child knows from repeated encounters with the book exactly what the text on each page says, the child realizes that something isn't working right, that print and speech must relate differently than the way the child first supposed. Thus, the mismatch is likely to lead to the testing of a different strategy.

Perhaps this time the child points to groups of letters marked by space (words in print) as syllables are said. This strategy works well unless some of the words in the text have more than one syllable. For example, this strategy results in an even match between print and speech if the title of the book *Where the Wild Things Are* is being read, but not if the title of the book being read is *The Very Hungry Caterpillar.*

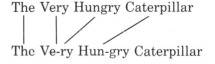

Where the Wild Things Are   (text)

Where the Wild Things Are   (verbalization with fingerpointing)

The Very Hungry Caterpillar   (text)

The Ve-ry Hun-gry Caterpillar   (verbalization with fingerpointing)

In the second case, where a mismatch occurs, the child runs out of print to point to before all of the words that are expected to be there are said. Again, the mismatch serves as a clue to the child that the strategy selected must be modified.

Experiments of this kind typically continue for many months before the child discovers and masters the actual relationship between print and speech. There may be periods when the child stops trying to match speech to print exactly, and just reads the stories without pointing to the print. Then, a bit later, the child returns again to try to figure out how print works.

Other experiences in addition to story reading no doubt influence children's progress in matching speech to print. For example, learning how their name is written, or dictating stories to be written down by an adult, surely help.

The advantage of picture books is that they provide many different samples of print with which children can experiment. Dictated stories can also provide many print samples, but it is difficult for children to remember exactly what they said while dictating. Thus, if print and speech do not match up later when the story is read, the child can attribute the error to her or his oral rendering instead of to incorrect matching. The story often gets changed a bit so that text and speech come out even.

But with picture books, the oral rendition is often known very well before an interest in print emerges. It is difficult for children to alter a story when they have heard it read in exactly the same way time after time, over a period of months, or even years. In this situation, they are very sure of what the print should say, and thus more likely to change their mapping strategy than the story. It is for this reason that mapping speech to print in storybooks may lead to more experimenting with mapping per se than does mapping speech to print in other situations.

Learning that written language and oral language differ

Written language differs from oral language in style. For example, written language is more formal and more complete.

> Normal spoken language is . . . a kind of composite message coming from language in association with sensory context. In consequence, spoken language structures may be incomplete or ambiguous in themselves without being confusing, because the situation adds its own components to the meaning. Written language cannot afford to be incomplete in these ways—it must carry the *total* load of meaning without ambiguity. This is the main reason why the written dialect is so different from conversational language. It is more formal, more complete, and more textured than spoken language, and to avoid ambiguity it has distinctive structures which do not appear in spoken dialects. (Holdaway, 1979, p. 54).

Written language carries more of the burden of meaning by itself. While readers always take meaning *to* a text, there is a very real sense in which the meaning is also carried by the text in a way that it is not in a spoken utterance. This has implications for the task of learning to read.

> When children are taught to read, they are learning both to read and to treat language as text. Children familiar with the use of textlike language through hearing printed stories obviously confront less of a hurdle than those for whom both reading and that form of language are novel. (Olson, 1980, p. 103)

Teale (1984) suggests that in addition to learning how to understand text versus conversation, children learn specific ways of "taking from text" (p. 117). For example, he notes that in studies of parental book-reading episodes, some parents use a "life-to-text interaction" pattern. In other words, we help children understand stories when we relate the story events to the child's own life.

There are, no doubt, other patterns of "taking from text" that influence how children learn to comprehend text. We are only now beginning to study these aspects of the story-reading situation, and we do not yet know how adult reading varies in these respects, or what effect various patterns have on children's later literacy skills.

Learning the culture of school

In addition to learning "book language" and how to take meaning from text, story-reading experience may teach children school dialogue patterns and other school-related behaviors, if parents or preschool teachers use patterns similar to those found in the primary school. For example, in a study of parental reading to preschool children in three different communities, Heath (1982) found that middle-class parents asked a lot of *why* questions, similar to the kinds of questions children face in school. The greater school success of middle-class children may be due in part to their greater familiarity with this pattern of interaction—this way of behaving—which is different from what children know. This kind of knowledge is described well by Mehan (1982):

> To be effective in the classroom, students must indeed master academic subject matter. . . . But effective participation in the classroom is not limited to academic matters. Although it is incumbent on students to display *what* they know, they also must know *how* to display their knowledge. (p. 79)

When the dialogue patterns we use when reading to children are similar to those used in school, children gain something more

We help children understand stories when we relate the story events to the child's own life.

Robert Meier

than knowledge about books. They also learn how to relate their knowledge in a school setting. The often reported relationship between preschool story-reading experience (and preschool experience in general) and academic success may be due in part to this kind of learning.

Knowing that reading leads to enjoyment

A final contribution of story-reading experience is the pleasure that it can bring. Hearing stories can be a very interesting experience for children. Stories tell of other children, animals, funny situations, and of frightening events that typically turn out all right. Being able to enter into the world of stories on their own is something that many children want to do, once they have experienced the joy that stories can bring. Thus, experience with stories can build a positive attitude toward reading and can develop a strong desire to learn to read.

Aside from the interest that early story reading can build for stories themselves, there is probably an emotional component of the experience in the positive, personal interaction between adult and child. Story reading often takes place in an adult's lap or beside the parent as parent and child sit on the child's bed. The bedtime story may be one of the most positive times of the day for both parent and child, especially if a bedtime story is a ritual. Adult and child know what the routine is, so the negotiation that characterizes other activities during the day is not present. The book, as the basis for interaction, makes it easy to talk together. And the prospect of soon having a few hours without the many necessary interruptions that come with caring for young children may make parents particularly calm and nurturant during story-reading time. In addition, story reading is often wrapped up with the goodnight kiss and the tucking-in ritual, which are very nurturing and positive interactions.

Taylor (1983) relates the strong feelings about story reading one parent experienced. One day the mother bought a copy of *Peter Rabbit* in French for her teenager. The two of them spent a long time reading it and comparing it with English versions of the story they had in the house. In relating the event, the mother commented that she would hold onto the memories of that evening

Chapter 3

If experience with books is enjoyable, and if it occurs under especially nurturant conditions, the feelings associated with reading and books are likely to be highly positive.

for a long time. She then commented about life with a teenager and what the book event had meant to her:

> It was a marvelous evening.... [A]t this age they shun physical affection although they still need some, and you have to tease them into it a bit. Just to be able to give them a kiss now and then. That night I tucked her into bed and she said *"Goodnight."* She didn't say, *"Oh, mother!"* It was gone just for that night. To be able to go back. (p. 83)

As Taylor summarizes, "the seemingly benign literate activity of reading bedtime stories to the preschool child can permeate years of family life" (p. 83). It probably permeates years of school life, too. If experience with books is enjoyable, and if it occurs under especially nurturant conditions, the feelings associated with reading and books are likely to be highly positive. The development of such positive attitudes toward books and reading may be one of the most important contributions that early book-reading experiences can make.

Development of story-reading behavior

Children's storybook behavior changes over the course of the preschool years if children are provided with frequent experiences with books. A child's behavior with books depends on

1. the child's past experience with books in general, and with the book in hand in particular,

2. the child's current understanding of the function of print, print conventions, and characteristics of the orthography, and

3. the structure of the book.

For example, we would expect a 4-year-old who had been read to almost daily since babyhood to behave differently than one who had been read to only rarely, and we would expect a 4-year-old to behave differently when hearing a book for the first time than when hearing it for the 20th time. Furthermore, a child who knows that print is read, not the pictures, is likely to behave differently than a child who still assumes that the pictures are read, or that the print cannot be read without reference to the pictures. And, finally, a 4-year-old would be expected to behave differently when hearing two books that differ as much as do *The Very Hungry Caterpillar* and *Cinderella*, because one has a very simple, predictable text, while the other does not.

Some of the variations we observe in story-reading behavior are child characteristics—knowledge the child does or does not have due to past experience and perhaps general style of learning or learning ability. But others, such as the newness of a particular book and its structure, are situation-specific. So when we talk about the development of story-reading behavior, we must keep in mind that behavior is different for the *same child* when situations differ. Despite situation-based variations, however, children do exhibit some general developmental trends in story-reading behavior as their experience with books increases.

Accuracy in retelling stories

The accuracy of a child's retellings of books is influenced by four factors: the characteristics of the child's language, structure

Developmental trends in children's story-reading behavior

1. Children become increasingly able to retell the text more accurately.

2. Children move from thinking the pictures are read to knowing print can be read without reference to the pictures.

3. Once they are aware of and interested in print, children develop a more accurate understanding of how the orthography and speech relate. They map speech and print more accurately.

4. Children change from having almost complete interest in the pictures and the meaning of the story to interest in features of the text.

of the book, familiarity with the book, and past experience with books in general.

Oral language. If the child is very young, but has had considerable experience hearing simple, repetitive texts, the child's retellings will reflect her or his immature grammar and speech. For example, an 18-month-old boy retold certain pages of his favorite books. When hearing *The Cat in the Hat* (Seuss, 1957), he delighted in saying *"Ish, No! No!"* on the page that reads:

> But our fish said, *"No! No!"*
> Make that cat go away!
> Tell that Cat in the Hat
> You do not want to play. (unpaged)

He also liked to try to repeat the following lines from the same book:

> Bump! Thump! Bump! Thump!
> Down the wall in the hall. (unpaged)

In addition, he became very excited in anticipating the four repetitions of "Sit!" found on the third page of that book.

Three characteristics of these retellings are interesting here. First, at this point of development, the child selected to retell (or chime in on) passages that matched his own oral language patterns, which included some holophrases and many two- to four-word sentences. The texts he liked most to repeat contained single words (No! No! Sit! Sit! Sit! Sit! Bump! Thump!), the use of which he had recently mastered.

Secondly, when he tried to repeat multiword utterances, he changed them to fit the grammar characteristic of his own, immature, oral language. He did not say, "But our fish said, 'No! No!'" He said *"—ish, No! No!"* And he said only *"Down wall an hall,"* for "Down the wall in the hall."

Third, his articulation of words from the text was similar to his articulation in conversation. For example, he omitted the *f* in *fish*.

The constraints the child's grammar and articulation place on story retelling are less apparent in preschool children than in toddlers, because their language development has progressed much further. But irregular verbs in the past tense, for example, are changed to past tense in accordance with the rules for the regular verbs. Thus, the word *felt* in a line from *The Very Hungry Caterpillar* is changed to *feeled* by most preschoolers when they retell the story.

Children who speak a dialect will translate standard English texts into their dialect during retellings. And preschool children who are learning English as a second language will retell a text using the grammar that is typical of their development in the second language.

In all of these cases, the child's accuracy in retelling a story will increase over time, not simply because a story will have been heard many more times, but because the child's oral language development will become more mature or more like standard forms similar to those found in story texts.

Predictability of the text. The structure of the book the child retells will also influence the accuracy of the retelling. Predictable books (Rhodes, 1981) have texts that are especially easy to anticipate and recall. Several characteristics, such as the presence of repetition and rhyme, make books predictable.

Goodnight Moon is a highly predictable book because of both repetition and rhyme. For example, consider the following segments of text from this book:

> In the great green room
> There was a telephone
> And a red balloon
> And a cow jumping over the moon. (unpaged)

> Goodnight room.
> Goodnight moon.
> Goodnight cow jumping over the moon. (unpaged)

The kind of sentence used stays basically the same throughout many parts of the book. Just a few words, such as *room, moon,* and *cow jumping over the moon,* are changed. And the verses throughout the book rhyme.

In *The Very Hungry Caterpillar* (Carle, 1969) we find extensive use of repetitive sentences, with word substitutions. For example, the text goes like this:

> On Monday he ate one apple.
> But he was still hungry. (p. 6)

> On Tuesday he ate two pears, but
> he was still hungry. (p. 7)

The story continues through the days of the week. The name of the day changes, as does the number and the type of food, but the sentence pattern stays the same, which makes the book highly predictable.

Repetition and rhyme are very common in books for young children. Apparently authors of children's books have known for a long time that even young children like to retell stories, and they have structured books to make this possible.

Familiarity with the book. All other things being equal, the more a child has heard a story, the greater is the probability that the child's retelling of the story will be accurate. Sometimes, only a few readings of a highly predictable book, such as *The Very Hungry Caterpillar,* are required to enable a child to retell the story pretty accurately. Other books that are less predictable, or

---

As children first become acquainted with books as infants, toddlers, and preschoolers, they learn

1. How books work.
2. Print should make sense.
3. Print and speech are related in a specific way.
4. Book language differs from speech.
5. Patterns of interacting characteristic of behaviors expected in a school setting.
6. Books are enjoyable.

---

longer, require many rereadings before the child can retell the story accurately.

Any adult who has read to preschool children very much has no doubt noticed how much children like to have the same story repeated over and over again. Sometimes a child goes on a binge with one or two books, and wants these read repeatedly for a period of several weeks. Children may ask to have a story repeated many times so they can learn it by heart and then be able to read it themselves.

Experience with books in general. General book experience influences the accuracy of retellings in several ways. First, it increases the child's familiarity with book language. Greater familiarity with book language increases the accuracy of reading any specific book.

Second, a child's concepts about what is involved in reading a book also change with experience. Children with less experience are less likely than children with more experience to realize that the reader reads the print, not the pictures, and that the print is stable, that what is there stays the same. Children seem to realize with more experience that each book has its own story, a specific story, which remains the same each time the book is read, and that the story is told in specific words (Rossman, 1980). Accuracy of retellings, then, may be influenced by changes in children's concepts about what reading a book involves. If a child thinks that reading a story means telling a story that goes with the pictures, the child's retellings are not likely to match the text.

> # A decrease in a child's willingness to tell a story may indicate an increase in the child's understanding about the exactness and stability of the story.

But if a child thinks that reading a story means saying exactly the same words that are in the book, then a child's retellings may be very accurate.

A child's willingness to retell stories—to read to you—may depend on the child's concept of what reading a story means, as well as on the child's judgment of her or his ability to read a particular story in a way that is consistent with this concept. For example, in a study of preschoolers' story-reading behavior, children naive in terms of book experience were often willing to create a story by looking at the book's illustrations. Children somewhat more experienced would not make up a story, but were willing to tell the story in their own words. Children even more experienced, however, told the story exactly and asked about the words they did not know. When confronted with an unfamiliar story, they often refused to retell it and usually said, *"I don't know the words in that one; you read it"* (Rossman, 1980).

Sometimes adults view with some dismay the reluctance of children to read books, especially if they have done so willingly in the past. But a decrease in a child's willingness to tell a story may indicate an increase in the child's understanding about the exactness and stability of the story that is printed in a book. Reluctance, in this case, indicates progress, not regression.

Awareness of print

Young preschoolers seem to think that a reader looks at pictures to know what a book says. But as children gain more experience, they begin to realize that it is the print, not the pictures, that a reader reads.

Sometimes children's behavior in the story-reading situation is determined by their views about the function of print versus pictures. For example, some books have pages with pictures but no print, such as *Rosie's Walk* and *Where the Wild Things Are.* Children who think pictures tell the story often request the reader to read the textless pages, and tell them they forgot to read a page. They may even seem puzzled when the reader explains that those pages cannot be read, because they have no words.

More experienced children, however, may comment spontaneously about the fact that the textless pages cannot be read because they have no words. Some children even watch very closely to see when the next pages with print are reached and tell the reader, *"Now you can read again. The words have started."*

Sometimes children who think pictures tell the story hold a book so the print is covered. They are so unaware of the function of the print that they may need to be asked to move their hands out of the way on almost every page if they are holding the book. Older children, in contrast, know at once what the problem is when it is called to their attention, and they typically move their hand quickly and say something like, *"Oops, I forgot."* Some older preschoolers, who like to tease, may cover the print on purpose to play a trick on the adult. They laugh and know very well that the adult cannot continue until they move their hand.

Adults can quickly determine whether a child thinks the reader reads pictures or print by asking some simple questions: *"Where should I look to start to read this book?"* or *"Where do you think my eyes look while I read a book? Show me."* Younger children invariably point to the pictures instead of to the print.

Somewhat older children often point to the print, although they may point to the pictures, too, and say something such as, *"You look at the pictures to know what the words say."* In this case, children may be saying they are aware of the print, but pictures are needed. They may not be aware that print can function independently of pictures to tell a story, or they may be saying *they* need both, that the pictures help them remember what the print on a page says. For additional discussion of how young children come to view the function of pictures versus print, see Ferreiro (1979).

More accurate print/speech matching

Attempts to match the oral telling of a story with the print in the book appear relatively late in the development of storybook behavior. This makes sense because print/speech matching behavior depends on development of the first two trends that we have discussed. Without awareness of print in a book, for example, children would not attempt to match it to speech.

First attempts to match speech to print are global. A child may sweep back and forth across the print, indicating that she or he knows in general that all of the print represents what is being said. The child seems not to realize that the print has parts or that these relate in any specific way to the utterance. Global sweeping also may be largely imitative. Adults often run a finger along under the text while reading it. Children may notice this and include it in their story-reading behavior.

Once children do begin to try to match parts of the text to specific utterances, a new developmental era has begun. It is a lengthy era, however, for the understandings that underlay accurate matching are difficult, as we have already mentioned. A child usually experiments for many months before the puzzle is completely solved. And solving it requires that children know some samples of print very, very well. Highly predictable books and books in which the pictures match the story very well are helpful, even necessary. It is necessary, too, for children to have time to look at books, to have time to read to themselves or to a friend. Books must be available to children, not kept on shelves only for adults to read *to* children, if children are to have a chance to discover how print works.

Interest in features of the text

Toddlers and young preschoolers often ask many questions during a story-reading session: *"Where's his mommy?" "Why he sad?"* But as children master the messages in their storybooks, and as they begin to become aware of the print, their questions often shift from ones about the story to ones about the print. With an older experienced preschooler, it sometimes seems that the story as such is hardly of any interest. Instead, the child asks questions such as *"What does this word say?"* or *"Where does it say ... ?"* Or children may search for a certain word, such as the name of a character in the story. At this point, familiarity with the book serves as a scaffold for the child's explorations of the print. Knowing a story by heart and knowing how to match speech with print enables a child to locate many words and to study their features.

Of course, new books with unfamiliar stories will often shift attention back to questions about characters, motives, and feelings; and new events in a child's life may lead to new questions about old stories. Nevertheless, a shift has occurred, and the adult is now likely to entertain as many questions about the print as about the story.

Story reading in group programs

We have seen in this chapter how extremely important the story-reading experience is to literacy development. Perhaps no other activity contributes so much. How, then, can we support story reading and exploration of books in excellent programs for young children? What can we do to ensure children access to good books and stories?

Display of books

All of the recommendations about how children's books can be made most accessible are based on these assumptions: Books are kept in a special book area in the room, the room is organized into learning centers, and the schedule includes an extended period for free-choice activities.

Type of books. Books offered to young children should be good quality children's literature, including some highly predictable books like those listed in Table 3.1. You will want to include some familiar books, a couple of relatively new ones, a few that are very simple, and some that are more complex. A variety of topics should be represented in the books because children's interests will vary. It is also nice to include books that have been made by the children, and perhaps a photo album of school events, with captions that explain what each photo depicts.

Appeal of display. The way books are displayed influences the area's attractiveness and children's interest in spending time there. It is a good idea for teachers to stand back and take a good look at the book area. Does the book display look interesting? Colorful?

A small, cozy book center attracts children more than a larger center.

Uncluttered? Can a child who enters the area find a specific book without having to search? Are book covers visible? If your display rack does not hold books so the covers show, stand a limited number of books open on the shelf.

Teachers might also evaluate the book center in terms of physical and emotional comfort. Is there a child-sized rocker in the area? Are there pillows? Is the area carpeted? Is the area small and cozy, or is it so large that it does not appear to be a protected, special place? Rawson and Goetz (1983) report that a small, cozy book center attracts children more than a larger center.

Care of books. The books included in a center should always be complete and well cared for. When pages are torn, teachers can help children mend them with tape. When books are worn out, they should be removed.

Attention to all of these details will help to make the book area a favorite place of the children.

Support for story reading

Although the physical characteristics of the book corner are important, these alone are not enough. Teachers must support the area with their behavior if children are to use the area productively.

It is not uncommon to visit preschool classrooms during activity time and observe that teachers never enter the book area. Adults tend to supervise art or cooking projects or get materials ready for an activity later in the day. Because the book center is not an area where safety or messiness are issues, and because most programs have a group storytime scheduled for each day, teachers tend to ignore the book area during activity time. But because children benefit so much from being close to the book when it is read, from having their favorite stories reread many times, and from having their questions answered, the book center is an important place for teachers to try to spend some of their time.

Teachers cannot, and need not, spend an inordinate amount of time in the book area. In one study, for example, children chose to go to the book corner more when teachers were there intermittently, rather than when they never were there, or were there all of the time (Rawson & Goetz, 1983). In short, children spend the most time in the book corner during activity time when a teacher is there once in a while.

Why are children's visits to the book corner linked to the amount of time a teacher spends there? When teachers are never in the book area, children who need the close emotional support of an adult to explore an area the first few times, before they explore it on their own, may never venture into the book area.

Secondly, children often wish to greet teachers upon arriving for the day and often want to share experiences with them throughout the day. This means that children often will go to where a teacher is present, just to be able to talk with the teacher. But upon arrival to an area, the child often notices what is going on, or may even be invited by the teacher to join in. As a result, children are systematically exposed to certain areas of the room and not to others, if teachers systematically station themselves in the same places. There may be a particular temptation for teachers to station themselves in areas other than the book corner because it is not messy or dangerous. But this may not be wise if teachers want to encourage children to use books.

A third reason why total teacher absence from the book corner may inhibit its use is because much of the enjoyment children gain when looking at books independently may come when children are familiar with the books from prior story reading. If an adult never reads the books, or reads each one very infrequently during a large group storytime, children simply may not gain much pleasure from looking at the books by themselves.

But why might constant teacher presence diminish visits to a book corner? Of course, there is no way to know for sure, but we can guess that the book area, especially a small and cozy one, is a comfortable place for children to go when they wish to be by themselves. If adults are ever-present, children are likely to seek other places to enjoy some privacy.

Children spend the most time in the
book corner during activity time when
a teacher is there once in a while.

In addition, when children are practicing some of their emerging reading abilities, they may prefer at times to do this out of earshot of an adult. For example, in a study conducted by Rossman (1980), children seemed to enter a no-response phase when asked to read a book to the researcher, at just about the time they were moving from one way of reading books to a higher level. In Rossman's study, these children asked the researcher to read the books and refused to read them by themselves. This may indicate that children are particularly sensitive about reading books when they think they need to change the way they have been doing it. If alone, however, they may feel safe enough to practice. Even children who are not struggling to attain a new level of book-reading behavior may enjoy some peace and quiet from time to time in the book area, rather than the constant sound of the voice of an adult reader who may forget that the animated and projected voice that is so effective for group story reading is unnecessary and somewhat annoying in the quiet space of a cozy book corner.

Intermittent reading, for all of the reasons given above, may serve all of the children best. You might consider spending a few short periods in the book center throughout each daily activity period, or make certain to visit it several times a week, as the schedule allows.

You might also try to include a listening center as part of the book area, or adjacent to it. A tape recorder or record player with a listening post and headphones can extend the story-listening opportunities available to children during activity time. Even three or four stories with tapes add considerably to the classroom.

You may want to cover paperback books that often come with tapes with clear contact paper to ensure they will last a long time, because they tend to be used a lot. Children can learn how to use the tape recorder or record player independently, or with very little assistance. Of course, machines do not answer children's questions, but they can take the place of a teacher for part of the time.

The story-reading corner is also a place where auxiliary staff can be of help. Almost all adults know what to do and therefore feel comfortable in the book center. High school or other volunteers often like to spend some time in the book area, and time spent there certainly can benefit the children.

In summary, it is important to try to give the book center equal billing during free-choice time. It certainly is no more important for children to look at books and listen to stories than it is for them to play house, paint, play in water or sand, and build with blocks. But it is just as important. And because it is, we should try to make certain that we support, rather than ignore, book reading, which we sometimes do because it does not seem to need our attention in the direct way that other areas of the classroom do.

References

Brown, M. W. (1947). *Goodnight moon.* New York: Harper & Row.

Carle, E. (1969). *The very hungry caterpillar.* Cleveland: Collins.

Clark, M. M. (1976). *Young fluent readers.* London: Heinemann.

Doake, D. (1981). *Book experience and emergent reading in preschool children.* Unpublished doctoral dissertation, University of Alberta, Edmonton.

Durkin, D. (1966). *Children who read early.* New York: Teachers College Press, Columbia University.

Ferreiro, E., & Teberosky, A. (1979). *Literacy before schooling.* Portsmouth, NH: Heinemann.

Goodman, K. S., & Goodman, Y. M. (1980). Learning about psycholinguistic processes by analyzing oral reading. In M. Wolf, M. K. McQuillan, & E. Radwin (Eds.), *Thought and language/language and reading.* Cambridge, MA: Harvard University Press.

Heath, S. B. (1982). What no bedtime story means: Narrative skills at home and school. *Language in Society, 11,* 49–76.

Holdaway, D. (1979). *The foundations of literacy.* New York: Ashton Scholastic.

Hutchins, P. (1968). *Rosie's walk.* New York: Macmillan.

Liberman, I. Y., Shankweiler, D., Fischer, F. W., & Carter, B. (1974). Explicit syllable and phoneme segmentation in the young child. *Journal of Experimental Child Psychology, 18,* 201–212.

Mason, J. (1980). When do children begin to read: An exploration of four year old children's letter and word reading competencies. *Reading Research Quarterly, 15,* 203–227.

Mehan, H. (1982). The structure of classroom events and their consequences for student performance. In P. Gilmore & A. A. Glatthorn (Eds.), *Children in and out of school: Ethnography and education.* Washington, DC: Center for Applied Linguistics.

Menyuk, P. (1976). Relations between acquisition of phonology and reading. In J. T. Guthrie (Ed.), *Aspects of reading acquisition.* Baltimore, MD: Johns Hopkins University Press.

Olson, D. R. (1980). From utterance to text: The bias of language in speech and writing. In M. Wolf, M. K. McQuillan, & E. Radwin (Eds.), *Thought and language/language and reading.* Cambridge, MA: Harvard University Press.

Plessas, G. P., & Oakes, C. R. (1964). Prereading experiences of selected early readers. *The Reading Teacher, 17,* 241–245.

Rawson, R. M., & Goetz, E. M. (1983). *Reading-related behavior in preschoolers: Environmental factors and teacher modeling.* Unpublished manuscript.

Rhodes, L. K. (1981). I can read! Predictable books as resources for reading and writing instruction. *The Reading Teacher, 34,* 511–518.

Rossman, F. (1980). *Preschoolers' knowledge of the symbolic function of written language in storybooks.* Unpublished doctoral dissertation, Boston University.

Schickedanz, J. A. (1978, July). "Please read that story again!": Exploring relationships between story reading and learning to read. *Young Children, 33*(5), 43–55.

Schickedanz, J. A., & Sullivan, M. (1984). Mom, what does u-f-f spell? *Language Arts, 61*(1), 7–17.

Sendak, M. (1963). *Where the wild things are.* New York: Scholastic.

Seuss, Dr. (1957). *The cat in the hat.* New York: Random House.

Smith, F. (1983). *Essays into literacy.* Cambridge: Cambridge University Press.

Sutton, M. H. (1964). Readiness for reading at the kindergarten level. *The Reading Teacher, 17,* 234–240.

Taylor, D. (1983). *Family literacy: Young children learning to read.* Portsmouth, NH: Heinemann.

Taylor, I. (1981). Writing systems and reading. In G. E. MacKinnon & T. G. Waller (Eds.), *Reading research: Advances in theory and practice* (Vol. 2). New York: Academic.

Teale, W. H. (1984). Reading to young children: Its significance for literacy development. In H. Goelman & A. Oberg (Eds.), *Awakening to literacy* (pp. 110–121). Exeter, NH: Heinemann.

Wells, G. (1981). *Learning through interaction: The study of language development.* Cambridge: Cambridge University Press.

Suggested books for preschoolers

There are dozens of good books for preschool children. The list which follows includes some of the best books, but it is by no means exhaustive.

Ahlberg, A., & Ahlberg, J. (1978). *Each peach pear plum.* New York: Scholastic.

Asbjorsin, P. (1973). *The three billy goats gruff.* New York: Houghton Mifflin.

Asch, F. (1982). *Happy birthday moon.* Englewood Cliffs, NJ: Prentice-Hall.

Barton, B. (1989). *Dinosaurs, dinosaurs.* New York: Thomas Crowell.

Carle, E. (1974). *The very hungry caterpillar.* New York: Philomel.

dePaola, T. (1981). *Now one foot. Now the other.* New York: Putnam.

Dowell, P. (1991). *Zoo animals.* New York: Macmillan.

Ehlert, L. (1990). *Feathers for lunch.* Orlando, FL: Harcourt Brace Jovanovich.

Ehlert, L. (1990). *Fish eyes.* Orlando, FL: Harcourt Brace Jovanovich.

Ets, M. H. (1963). *Gilberto and the wind.* New York: Viking.

Freeman, D. (1968). *Corduroy.* New York: Viking.

Galdone, P., illustrator. (1968). *Henny Penny.* New York: Seabury.

Hoban, R. (1960). *Bedtime for Frances.* New York: Harper & Row.

Keats, E. J. (1979). *Over in the meadow.* New York: Parents Magazine Press.

Keats, E. J. (1968). *A letter to Amy.* New York: Harper & Row.

McCloskey, R. (1948). *Blueberries for Sal.* New York: Penguin.

McCloskey, R. (1941). *Make way for ducklings.* New York: Penguin.

Potter, B. (1902). *The tale of Peter Rabbit.* New York: Frederick Warne.

Sendak, M. (1963). *Where the wild things are.* New York: Scholastic.

Seuss, Dr. (1957). *The cat in the hat.* New York: Random House.

Slobodkina, E. (1947). *Caps for sale.* Reading, MA: Addison-Wesley.

Viorst, J. (1977). *Alexander and the terrible, horrible, no good, very bad day.* New York: Atheneum.

Table 3.1
Predictable Books
A bibliography of predictable books

Adams, Pam. *This Old Man*. New York, N.Y.: Grossett and Dunlap, 1974.

Alain. *One, Two, Three, Going to Sea*. New York, N.Y.: Scholastic, 1964.

Aliki. *Go Tell Aunt Rhody*. New York, N.Y.: Macmillan, 1974.

Aliki. *Hush Little Baby*. Englewood Cliffs, N.J.: Prentice-Hall, 1968.

Aliki. *My Five Senses*. New York, N.Y.: Thomas Y. Crowell, 1962.

Asch, Frank. *Monkey Face*. New York, N.Y.: Parents' Magazine Press, 1977.

Balian, Lorna. *The Animal*. Nashville, Tenn.: Abingdon Press, 1972.

Balian, Lorna. *Where in the World Is Henry?* Scarsdale, N.Y.: Bradbury Press, 1972.

Barohas, Sarah E. *I Was Walking Down the Road*. New York, N.Y.: Scholastic, 1975.

Baum, Arline, and Joseph Baum. *One Bright Monday Morning*. New York, N.Y.: Random House, 1962.

Becker, John. *Seven Little Rabbits*. New York, N.Y.: Scholastic, 1973.

Beckman, Kaj. *Lisa Cannot Sleep*. New York, N.Y.: Franklin Watts, 1969.

Beliah, Melanie. *A First Book of Sounds*. Racine, Wis.: Golden Press, 1963.

Bonne, Rose, and Alan Mills. *I Know an Old Lady*. New York, N.Y.: Rand McNally, 1961.

Brand, Oscar. *When I First Came to This Land*. New York, N.Y.: Putnam's Sons, 1974.

Brandenberg, Franz. *I Once Knew a Man*. New York, N.Y.: Macmillan, 1970.

Brown, Marcia. *The Three Billy Goats Gruff*. New York, N.Y.: Harcourt Brace Jovanovich, 1957.

Brown, Margaret Wise. *Four Fur Feet*. New York, N.Y.: William R. Scott, 1961.

Brown, Margaret Wise. *Goodnight Moon*. New York, N.Y.: Harper and Row, 1947.

Brown, Margaret Wise. *Home for a Bunny*. Racine, Wis.: Golden Press, 1956.

Brown, Margaret Wise. *Where Have You Been?* New York, N.Y.: Scholastic, 1952.

The Bus Ride, illustrated by Justin Wager. New York, N.Y.: Scott, Foresman, 1971.

Carle, Eric. *The Grouchy Ladybug.* New York, N.Y.: Thomas Y. Crowell, 1977.

Carle, Eric. *The Mixed Up Chameleon.* New York, N.Y.: Thomas Y. Crowell, 1975.

Carle, Eric. *The Very Hungry Caterpillar.* Cleveland, Ohio: Collins World, 1969.

Charlip, Remy. *Fortunately.* New York, N.Y.: Parents' Magazine Press, 1964.

Charlip, Remy. *What Good Luck! What Bad Luck!* New York, N.Y.: Scholastic, 1969.

Cook, Bernadine. *The Little Fish that Got Away.* Reading, Mass.: Addison-Wesley, 1976.

de Regniers, Beatrice Schenk. *Catch a Little Fox.* New York, N.Y.: Seabury Press, 1970.

de Regniers, Beatrice Schenk. *The Day Everybody Cried.* New York, N.Y.: The Viking Press, 1967.

de Regniers, Beatrice Schenk. *How Joe the Bear and Sam the Mouse Got Together.* New York, N.Y.: Parents' Magazine Press, 1965.

de Regniers, Beatrice Schenk. *The Little Book.* New York, N.Y.: Henry Z. Walck, 1961.

de Regniers, Beatrice Schenk. *May I Bring a Friend?* New York, N.Y.: Atheneum, 1972.

de Regniers, Beatrice Schenk. *Willy O'Dwyer Jumped in the Fire.* New York, N.Y.: Atheneum, 1968.

Domanska, Janina. *If All the Seas Were One Sea.* New York, N.Y.: Macmillan, 1971.

Duff, Maggie. *Jonny and His Drum.* New York, N.Y.: Henry Z. Walck, 1972.

Duff, Maggie. *Rum Pum Pum.* New York, N.Y.: Macmillan, 1978.

Emberley, Barbara. *Simon's Song.* Englewood Cliffs, N.J.: Prentice-Hall, 1969.

Emberly, Ed. *Klippity Klop.* Boston, Mass.: Little, Brown, 1974.

Ets, Marie Hall. *Elephant in a Well.* New York, N.Y.: The Viking Press, 1972.

Ets, Marie Hall. *Play with Me.* New York, N.Y.: The Viking Press, 1955.

Flack, Marjorie. *Ask Mr. Bear.* New York, N.Y.: Macmillan, 1932.

Galdone, Paul. *Henny Penny.* New York, N.Y.: Scholastic, 1968.

Galdone, Paul. *The Little Red Hen.* New York, N.Y.: Scholastic, 1973.

Galdone, Paul. *The Three Bears*. New York, N.Y.: Scholastic, 1972.

Galdone, Paul. *The Three Billy Goats Gruff*. New York, N.Y.: Seabury Press, 1973.

Galdone, Paul. *The Three Little Pigs*. New York, N.Y.: Seabury Press, 1970.

Ginsburg, Mirra. *The Chick and the Duckling*. New York, N.Y.: Macmillan, 1972.

Greenberg, Polly. *Oh Lord, I Wish I Was a Buzzard*. New York, N.Y.: Macmillan, 1968.

Hoffman, Hilde. *The Green Grass Grows All Around*. New York, N.Y.: Macmillan, 1968.

Hutchins, Pat. *Good-Night Owl*. New York, N.Y.: Macmillan, 1972.

Hutchins, Pat. *Rosie's Walk*. New York, N.Y.: Macmillan, 1968.

Hutchins, Pat. *Titch*. New York, N.Y.: Collier Books, 1971.

Keats, Ezra Jack. *Over in the Meadow*. New York, N.Y.: Scholastic, 1971.

Kent, Jack. *The Fat Cat*. New York, N.Y.: Scholastic, 1971.

Klein, Lenore. *Brave Daniel*. New York, N.Y.: Scholastic, 1958.

Kraus, Robert. *Whose Mouse Are You?* New York, N.Y.: Collier Books, 1970.

Langstaff, John. *Frog Went A-Courtin'*. New York, N.Y.: Harcourt Brace Jovanovich, 1955.

Langstaff, John. *Gather My Gold Together: Four Songs for Four Seasons*. Garden City, N.Y.: Doubleday, 1971.

Langstaff, John. *Oh, A-Hunting We Will Go*. New York, N.Y.: Atheneum, 1974.

Langstaff, John. *Over in the Meadow*. New York, N.Y.: Harcourt Brace Jovanovich, 1957.

Laurence, Ester. *We're Off to Catch a Dragon*. Nashville, Tenn.: Abingdon Press, 1969.

Lexau, Joan. *Crocodile and Hen*. New York, N.Y.: Harper and Row, 1969.

Lobel, Anita. *King Rooster, Queen Hen*. New York, N.Y.: Greenwillow, 1975.

Lobel, Arnold. *A Treeful of Pigs*. New York, N.Y.: Greenwillow, 1979.

Mack, Stan. *10 Bears in My Bed*. New York, N.Y.: Pantheon, 1974.

Martin, Bill. *Brown Bear, Brown Bear*. New York, N.Y.: Holt, Rinehart and Winston, 1970.

Martin, Bill. *Fire! Fire! Said Mrs. McGuire*. New York, N.Y.: Holt, Rinehart and Winston, 1970.

Mayer, Mercer. *If I Had . . . .* New York, N.Y.: Dial Press, 1968.

Mayer, Mercer. *Just for You*. New York, N.Y.: Golden Press. 1975.

McGovern, Ann. *Too Much Noise*. New York, N.Y.: Scholastic, 1967.

Memling, Carl. *Ten Little Animals*. Racine, Wis.: Golden Press, 1961.

Moffett, Martha. *A Flower Pot Is Not a Hat*. New York, N.Y.: E.P. Dutton, 1972.

Peppe, Rodney. *The House that Jack Built*. New York, N.Y.: Delacorte, 1970.

Polushkin, Maria. *Mother, Mother, I Want Another*. New York, N.Y.: Crown Publishers, 1978.

Preston, Edna Mitchell. *Where Did My Mother Go?* New York, N.Y.: Four Winds Press, 1978.

Quackenbush, Robert. *She'll Be Comin' Round the Mountain*. Philadelphia, Pa.: J.B. Lippincott, 1973.

Quackenbush, Robert. *Skip to My Lou*. Philadelphia, Pa.: J.B. Lippincott, 1975.

Rokoff, Sandra. *Here Is a Cat*. Singapore: Hallmark Children's Editions, no date.

Scheer, Jullian, and Marvin Bileck. *Rain Makes Applesauce*. New York, N.Y.: Holiday House, 1964.

Scheer, Jullian, and Marvin Bileck. *Upside Down Day*. New York, N.Y.: Holiday House, 1968.

Sendak, Maurice. *Where the Wild Things Are*. New York, N.Y.: Scholastic, 1963.

Shaw, Charles B. *It Looked Like Spilt Milk*. New York, N.Y.: Harper and Row, 1947.

Shulevitz, Uri. *One Monday Morning*. New York, N.Y.: Scribner's, 1967.

Skaar, Grace. *What Do the Animals Say?* New York, N.Y.: Scholastic, 1972.

Sonneborn, Ruth A. *Someone Is Eating the Sun*. New York, N.Y.: Random House, 1974.

Spier, Peter. *The Fox Went Out on a Chilly Night*. Garden City, N.Y.: Doubleday, 1961.

Stover, JoAnn. *If Everybody Did*. New York, N.Y.: David McKay, 1960.

Tolstoy, Alexei. *The Great Big Enormous Turnip*. New York, N.Y.: Franklin Watts, 1968.

Welber, Robert. *Goodbye, Hello*. New York, N.Y.: Pantheon, 1974.

Wildsmith, Brian. *The Twelve Days of Christmas*. New York, N.Y.: Franklin Watts, 1972.

Wolkstein, Diane. *The Visit*. New York, N.Y.: Alfred A. Knopf, 1977.

Wondriska, William. *All the Animals Were Angry*. New York, N.Y.: Holt, Rinehart and Winston, 1970.

Zaid, Barry. *Chicken Little*. New York, N.Y.: Random House, no date.

Zemach, Harve. *The Judge*. New York, N.Y.: Farrar, Straus and Giroux, 1969.

Zemach, Margot. *Hush, Little Baby*. New York, N.Y.: E.P. Dutton, 1976.

Zemach, Margot. *The Teeny Tiny Woman*. New York, N.Y.: Scholastic, 1965.

Zolotow, Charlotte. *Do You Know What I'll Do?* New York, N.Y.: Harper and Row, 1958.

From L. K. Rhodes. (1981). I can read! Predictable books as resources for reading and writing instruction. *The Reading Teacher, 34,* 511–518.

> Learning how to write involves much more than learning to write alphabet letters.

Chapter 4

Young Children and Writing

A 3-year-old accompanies his mother to the bank. She sets him up on the counter while she fills out a savings account withdrawal slip. The child watches intently and then asks, *"What you doing, Mommy?"*

The mother replies, *"I'm writing on this form so the cashier will know how much money I want to withdraw from my account."*

"I want to write one."

"Well, here, you can take this one home. We'll write it there. Other people need to use the counter now, and we are in the way."

The child holds on tightly to the withdrawal slip his mother gave him. Later, at home, his mother gives him a pencil, and he writes on his form. When he shows it to his mother, she says, *"Oh, let's see, you need $20. OK. Five, 10, 15, 20. Thank you."* She makes motions as if she is placing money in the child's hand.

As this episode suggests, preschoolers are fascinated with writing, with how adults do it, with the tools used for it, and with the

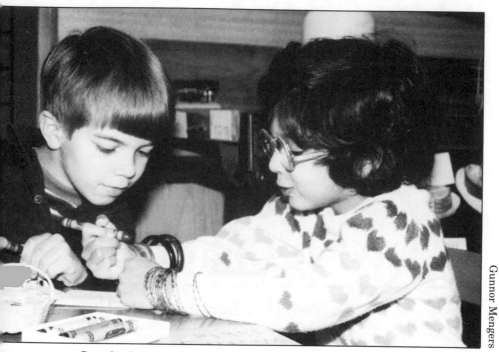

Preschoolers are fascinated with writing, with how adults do it, with the tools used for it, and with the results of their own efforts.

results of their own efforts. Many parents know how much young children love to write: We keep writing tools out of reach of the youngest children, except for times when their play can be supervised, because we know that if we don't, writing is likely to appear on walls, magazines, tables, and the floor.

Learning how to write involves much more than learning to write alphabet letters. Learning to write also involves knowing (1) how writing and speech relate, (2) how form and style vary depending on the situation, and (3) how a reader will react to what we have written. All of these skills depend on sophisticated and complex thinking, much of which is beyond preschoolers' abilities. Nevertheless, the beginnings of these skills can be found in preschool children. If teachers and parents recognize these beginnings, we can facilitate, rather than thwart, their development. In this chapter, we talk about the understandings that make up

---

Learning how to write involves learning

1. To write alphabet letters.
2. How writing and speech relate.
3. How form and style vary depending on the situation.
4. To predict how a reader will react to what we have written.

---

knowledge about writing, how young children's understanding of writing develops, and ways that we can support children's beginning efforts.

Learning to create print

Children's most obvious efforts to learn about writing center around physical and cognitive attempts to create marks that look like writing. While this is not all there is to writing, young children spend much time and effort on this task. We will spend considerable time, too, in an effort to understand what children do as they learn to create print.

Making letters

When children first attempt to create print, what they create may look like scribbles. Closer examination, however, usually shows that the scribbles have certain characteristics of print. They may be linear, rather than circular, and may be arranged horizontally more than vertically. They also may consist of repetitions of similar segments. These are the overall characteristics that children first use to judge whether or not marks are writing (Lavine, 1977), and also to create writing when they wish to write, rather than draw. In short, there is something very print-like, rather than picture-like, about these scribbles.

We can see quite clearly that children distinguish between drawing and writing when we look at a sample of each, produced by the same child, on the same piece of paper. Nora's pictures of a butterfly and her story about it appear in Figure 4.1. The part she said was her story certainly looks like writing, not like pictures, even though the writing contains no recognizable letters.

When children first attempt to create print, what they create may look like scribbles. Usually these scribbles have certain characteristics of print.

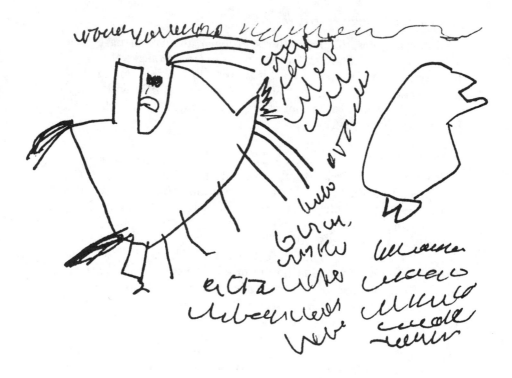

Figure 4.1. Nora's butterfly and her story (Schickedanz & Hultz, 1979).

Harste (1981) and his colleagues obtained many examples of this kind of differentiation in a study in which they asked children first to draw a picture of themselves and then to sign it with their name (Figure 4.2).

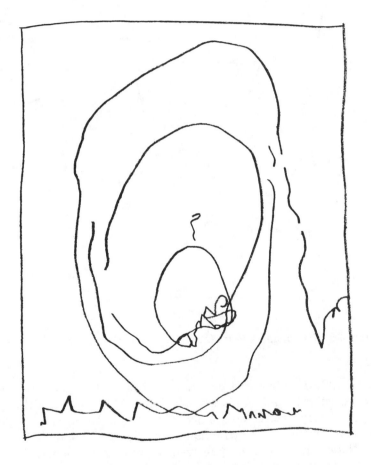

Figure 4.2. A picture (top) and the artist's signature (bottom), produced by a 3-year-old (Harste, Burke, & Woodward, 1981, p. 421).

Figure 4.3. Emma, age 4 years (Schickedanz & Molina, 1979).

As children gain more experience with writing they usually begin to write actual, or close approximations of, letters, although they still may use scribble much of the time. Often the two are combined, as they were by Emma, whose writing appears in Figure 4.3. Notice that a perfectly formed upper-case *E* appears in her writing sample, as does what appears to be an experiment with the lines used to make upper-case *E*s. Tawanna's writing sample (Figure 4.4) is similar. It is very common to find a letter from the child's name mixed in with scribble-writing (Clay, 1975).

Figure 4.4. Tawanna, age 3 years, 2 months (Holland, 1982).

As children become aware of how lines can be combined to form letters, many samples of their writing contain less scribble-writing, and more and more mock writing (letter-like forms) (Clay, 1975), combined with a few actual letters. Two samples of mock writing are shown in Figures 4.5 and 4.6. Figure 4.5 is a child's letter to Santa Claus. The story of *The Three Bears*, which this child wrote for her mother, is shown in Figure 4.6. Actual letters can be found in the story, although mock letters are more numerous.

Figure 4.5. Jose, age 4. A letter to Santa Claus (Schickedanz & Hultz, 1979).

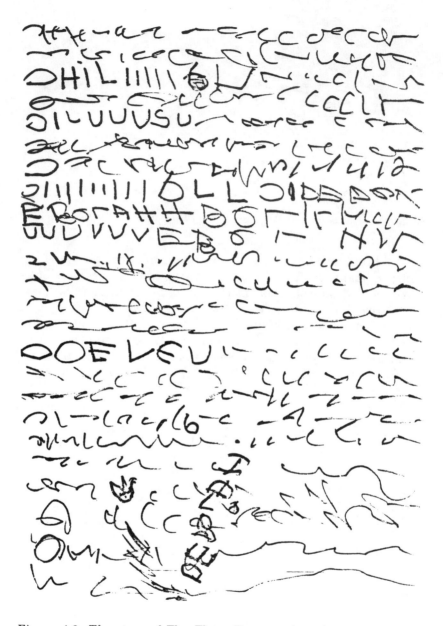

Figure 4.6. The story of The Three Bears, *written by a 4½-year-old (Schickedanz & Sullivan, 1984).*

The writing samples in Figures 4.7 and 4.8 show some progress beyond these figures. Here, only actual letters are used, although these are not without some errors. Matters such as orientation, the number of lines found in certain letters, and accuracy in making lines within a letter touch one another are not yet under complete control.

Figure 4.7. Writing produced by a 5-year-old (Schickedanz & Waldorf, 1980).

Figure 4.8. Writing produced by a 5-year-old (Schickedanz & Sullivan, 1984).

Figure 4.9. Paulette's display of ts *(Schickedanz & Molina, 1979).*

We do not know exactly how children gain complete accuracy in making letters, but it appears that at least some children do not achieve it only through practice in making letters correctly. In fact, there is evidence that children practice taking a letter to its extremes and comparing it with similar letters, perhaps to test just what effect variations in its lines and their orientation will have. Paulette, age 4, created the display of lower-case *t*s shown in Figure 4.9. We can see that she varied (1) the position at which the top horizontal line intersects the vertical line, (2) the lengths of both the horizontal and vertical lines, and (3) the orientation of the entire unit.

A similar experiment was conducted by Richard (Figure 4.10). The letter *R* was on his mind. Richard may have forgotten to add a line to an *R* in two instances, or he might have been trying to see just how a capital *R* and a capital *P* are the same and different.

A final example of a letter-making experiment is shown in Figure 4.11. Similar, but different, letters appear to have been compared in this case. All of the letters formed contain only straight vertical and horizontal lines.

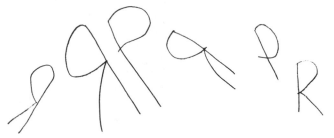

Figure 4.10. An experiment with the letter R. *Richard, age 2 years, 8 months (Holland, 1982).*

Figure 4.11 (Clay, 1975, p. 42).

81

Even when children can produce writing that resembles the standard form very closely, they often use scribble or mock-writing. Figure 4.12 shows the scribble-writing produced by a 4½-year-old. The child who produced it had been given a small notebook and a clipboard to take along to meetings she often attended with her mother. Her mother usually did a lot of writing at these meetings.

Figure 4.12. Scribble-writing created by a 4½-year-old imitating her mother's note-taking at a meeting (Schickedanz & Sullivan, 1983).

Subjects & Predicates

Part of learning to write involves learning how to organize writing on the paper. This problem is not as easy to master as it may seem, because it entails an understanding of spatial concepts.

Her daughter became interested in writing, too, and always took her supplies along. At the time this sample was produced, this child could write her name in standard form and could write *MOM* and *DAD*. But when she wanted to produce a lot of writing—imitate an adult while writing, or produce cursive writing—she often created scribble, rather than standard, writing. This behavior is quite typical; children do not discard earlier forms of writing altogether when they become capable of creating more mature forms. They select from among their expanding repertoire the style of writing that serves them best in each situation.

Organizing print in 2-dimensional space

Part of learning to write involves learning how to organize writing on the paper. This problem is not as easy to master as it may seem, because it entails an understanding of spatial concepts.

In much of children's early writing, vertical and horizontal placement are mixed. For example, while Emma and Tawanna (Figures 4.3 and 4.4) both used mainly vertically arranged scribble segments, they used horizontally placed segments as well. Furthermore, in many of the writing examples already given, orientation of the letters themselves is not consistent. Sometimes letters are reversed; sometimes they are placed upside-down. These characteristics, plus a tendency to write in any direction—left to right, right to left, top to bottom, bottom to top—are all related.

Until children understand that space can be organized in terms of coordinates, they do not select any consistent direction in which to place their writing, nor do they orient it consistently, one way or another. Mixed orientations are often found within the same writing sample. For example, when Sharon (Figure 4.13) ran out of room on her small piece of paper, after she wrote "I love you," she simply rotated the paper 180° and wrote *"Sharon,"* left to right, under her message. She did not seem to notice her completed sample contained two rows of writing whose orientations were inconsistent with each other.

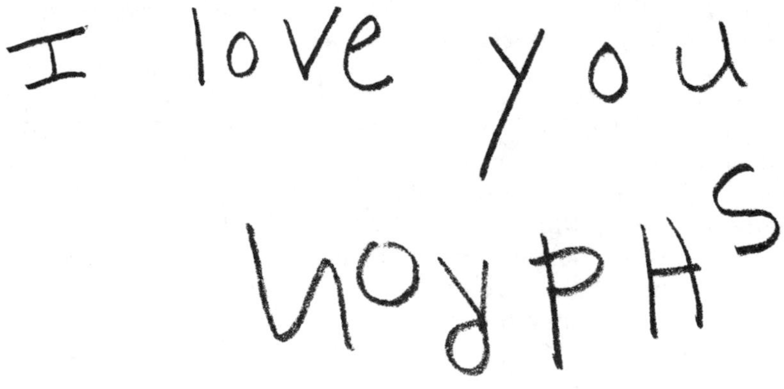

Figure 4.13. (Schickedanz & Molina, 1979).

Terrence (Figure 4.14), in contrast, knew how to solve the problem of running out of space on a line: Go to the left and begin another.

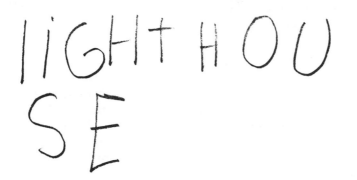

Figure 4.14. Terrence, age 6 years (Holland, 1982).

Sometimes when children write from right to left, they reverse each letter perfectly, as well, so that the writing produced is a mirror image of the standard left to right form (Figure 4.15). This kind of error shows a violation of accepted writing conventions

Figure 4.15. Mirror image writing produced by Claire, age 5 years, 6 months (Holland, 1982).

> # After children have played around with their own word dividers, they usually adopt the standard form.

(social agreements about the direction of writing), but a good understanding of spatial relations. A child who displays this level of skill in keeping directions and orientations consistent within a given sample of writing is probably ready to be reminded that *"we write from left to right."* However, there is no need to discourage a child who is experimenting with reversed writing.

Another, though quite unrelated, problem children have in organizing writing on a page has to do with leaving space between words. This omission is probably due to

1. lack of knowledge about what a word in speech is (compare *today* with *to go*),

2. lack of appreciation for the difficulty the reader who has no prior knowledge of the message will encounter (it's easier to read *IWATACT4MYBRTHDA* when it is written *I want a cat for my birthday)*, or

3. simple lack of knowledge about this writing convention.

A child who understands the first two conditions, but not the last one, often creates some way to separate words. For example, Paul, whose writing appears in Figure 4.16, used a dot to separate each word. Other children use dashes or slashes. When children create such devices, we can be relatively sure they will understand what we are talking about when we tell them space is used to separate one word from another. But again, we should not fuss when children wish to experiment with word dividers of their own making. Slashes, dashes, and dots work just fine for a while. After children have played around with these devices for a while, they usually adopt the standard form.

Learning how writing and speech relate

At the most basic level, children must discover what unit of speech is represented by the basic units of their orthography. In

Figure 4.16. Paul, age 5 years, 8 months (Bissex, 1980, p. 32).

English, each unit of the orthography—each letter—represents a phoneme in speech. After making this discovery, children must figure out just how the sounds of speech are coded by the orthography.

Discovering the basic unit of representation

We discussed this topic in Chapter 3, so we will not discuss it at length here. Children use the same hypotheses in trying to write as they use to relate speech to print in storybooks. For example, sometimes children create messages by writing one symbol (letter) for each word said. At other times they create one symbol for each syllable said. And at still other times, they create a lot of writing and just point globally to all of it as they "read" their message.

After much exploration, and after much exposure to print, children discover that letters represent phonemes, and not some larger unit of speech, such as a syllable or a word. This is a very important discovery. Once it is made, children must then learn to select

---

After much exploration and much exposure to print, children discover that letters represent phonemes. This is a very important discovery.

---

specific letters to represent what they wish to say. This, too, is difficult. We turn now to a discussion of how children approach this task.

Learning to write words

Many preschool teachers know that the words children first create when they try to represent words in terms of their sounds do not resemble conventional spellings. Children may write *kt* for *cat*, *grl* for *girl*, and *mdpi* for *mudpie*. What may not be readily apparent is how systematic these invented spellings are and how much they reveal children's keen ability to detect similarities and differences between the ways various sounds are produced.

The sounds we produce typically are described by speech experts in terms of articulation features. These features designate where in our mouth the sound is formed, whether it is formed quickly or slowly, and whether a sound is voiced or voiceless. When we compare any two sounds on a list of features, we find that sounds may be alike in some ways, but different in others. Table 4.1 compares the features of three sounds, [č] as in *church*, [t(r)] as in *trunk*, and [t] as in *toy*. As you can see, the sound of the *t* when it is followed by an *r*, as in the word *trunk,* shares the delay release and place of articulation features with the *č* sound found in *church,* and shares the distributed feature with the [t] sound found in *toy*. When forced to choose between the letters *ch* or *t* to represent a *t* before an *r*, children often opt for the *ch*. Thus, they spell words such as troubles and try like this: CHRIBLES and CHRIE (Read, 1975). Such spellings may look funny to us, but they certainly are understandable from a phonetic standpoint!

Table 4.1.
Articulation of [č], [t(r)], and [t] in English.

Feature	[č]	[t(r)]	[t]	Interpretation
delayed release	yes	yes	no	(affrication)
anterior	no	no	yes	(place of articulation)
distributed	yes	no	no	(type of contact)
retroflex	no	yes	no	(tongue shape)

(Adapted from Read, 1975, p. 53)

Other systematic errors include the substitution of one vowel for another. For example, tense, or what we often call long, vowels present no great problem to children because the letter names contain the sounds. Children used this relationship in spelling words such as face (FAS), came (Kam), and Coke (KOK) (Read, 1975). But the lax, or short, vowels are more difficult. What children seem to do is represent a lax vowel with the tense vowel that is most similar to it in terms of place of articulation. For example, children often represent the lax vowel found in words such as *fish*, *igloo*, *sink*, and *will* with an *e* rather than an *i*. But if you pronounce the sound represented by the letter *e* in a word, such as *eat*, and compare it to how your mouth feels when you pronounce a word like *dike*, you can see why children choose the *e* instead of the *i* in words like *fish* and *sink*. It is for the same reason that children often represent /E/ as in pen, mess, or teddy bear, with the letter *a* (pan, mas, taddebar) and /a/ as in got, box, and *upon*, with the letter *i* (GIT, BIGS, UPIN) (Read, 1975).

These examples illustrate that young children's spelling is not the result of poor listening. In fact, adults need to struggle to think about the creative relationships children detect. We have used standard spelling for so long that the *t*s in *truck* and *toy* sound very much alike to us, whereas the *ch* in *church* and the *t* in *truck* sound completely different.

Young children's spelling is not the result of poor listening. Exposing children to standard spelling found in storybooks; print in their environment; and classroom signs, labels, and charts is the way to help young children move in the direction of standard spellings.

Obviously, admonishing children to listen carefully as we pronounce words is not the way to help children solve this problem! **Exposing children to standard spelling found in storybooks; print in their environment; and classroom signs, labels, and charts is the way to help young children move in the direction of standard spellings.** Ways to provide this broad exposure to print are discussed in Chapter 5.

Learning to write for the situation

Suppose you received this imaginary letter in the mail:

Dear Helen,

> Once upon a time there was a frog named Hippity-Hop. He lived in a lake and sat on lily pads. One day he fell off of a lily pad, and that was the last time anyone saw him. Too bad!

> The End,

> Chris

> Even very young children become aware, through their experiences with print in various forms, of the difference between the form of a letter versus a story.

You would probably find such a letter amusing, for it contains writing that is more characteristic of stories than of letters!

What is particularly interesting about this situation is that it is very unlikely that we would receive such a letter, even from a very young child. Why? Very young children become aware, through their experiences with print in various forms, of the difference between the form of a letter versus a story. Four-year-old Megan, for example, knew this about writing, although she faltered at first with the form for the letter (Figure 4.17).

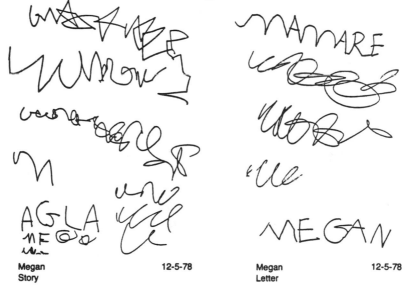

| Megan Story | 12-5-78 | Megan Letter | 12-5-78 |

Figure 4.17. (From Harste & Carey, 1979, p. 9).

In addition to knowing what to say when writing a letter versus writing a story, for example, young children quickly observe that writing is organized differently for different purposes. Children who write lists, for example, place the writing on the paper in a list-like array, but when they write a letter or a story, they include more writing on each line (Harste, 1983).

Learning to think about an audience

Writing, as we noted earlier in this book, differs from talking, because the sender and receiver of the message are usually separated from each other in time and space. Therefore, we must make our messages clear when we write, and we must supply all of the needed information. Sophisticated writers serve as writer and reader as they write; that is, they alternately move back and forth between both roles. Such mental flexibility requires advanced cognitive skills that do not become apparent until children are 9 or 10 years of age (Selman, 1971). Certainly, we cannot expect preschool children to stand back from and think about their writing in this way. However, there are situations that commonly arise in the classroom or at home that can help children begin to develop an awareness of audience.

Consider, for example, an activity in which one child is describing how to prepare peanut butter and jelly sandwiches. The teacher is writing the directions down on a piece of paper. The final version of the recipe will be drawn on a recipe chart to be used the following day when a small group of children will make peanut butter and jelly sandwiches for snack. The child explains the process like this:

"Well, first you take peanut butter and you put some on some bread. Then you push it around for a while. Then put jelly on some bread. That's all. Then you eat it."

"OK," says the teacher, after writing all of the child's dictation down, *"Let me see if I got this right. First you take peanut butter. Now, should that peanut butter be cold or room temperature?"*

"What?" asks the puzzled child.

"Well, I'm wondering if the peanut butter should be cold and hard, or warm and soft. It might be very hard to spread if it's cold. Where does your mom keep the peanut butter?"

"In the cupboard."

"Oh, then it would be room temperature; kind of warm."

"Right."

"Then you said that we should push the peanut butter around. Do you use something to push it with?"

"Yes, I use a knife. Well, it isn't really a knife. It's not sharp. It's sort of a spreader thing."

"Well we could say, 'Spread the peanut butter on the bread with a dull knife or spreader.'"

"OK."

"Now, how do you decide to stop spreading the peanut butter?"

"Well, you stop when it's all over the bread."

"I guess that's pretty obvious. Maybe we don't need to put that in."

"No, that's pretty easy."

"OK, then you said to put jelly on some bread. Do you mean that you spread jelly on a second slice of bread, just as you spread the peanut butter on the other slice?"

"Yes."

"OK. We can say, 'Spread jelly on a second slice of bread.' Then you said . . . no, you said that was it. But don't you have to put the two slices of bread together to make a sandwich?"

"Well, yes."

"Well, maybe we'd better say that. Some of the children who will be cooking may never have made sandwiches before. OK, we'll say, 'Place the slices of bread with jelly and peanut butter together to make a sandwich.' Then do you cut the whole thing into halves or fourths?"

"Sometimes, but you don't have to."

"Well, because our sandwiches are for snack instead of for lunch, we'd better cut them so they'll be small. Let's say, 'Cut into fourths.' OK?"

"OK."

"Now, let me read through all of this to see if we have it right. (Reads recipe.) How does that sound? Did we include everything?"

"Yes."

"OK. Thanks for going over this. I'll make a big chart for to-morrow."

The teacher in this situation helped the child think through his first dictation from the point of view of another child. The teacher acted as if she did not quite understand how the peanut butter sandwiches were to be made, much as a naive reader might actually do if she or he had requested a recipe from someone and was somewhat unsure of the directions given. In the process, details taken for granted by the writer were added so a naive reader would understand just what to do. In addition, a modification in the usual procedure was suggested (cutting the sandwiches into fourths) because the recipe was to be used to make sandwiches for snack.

The teacher in this illustration did a wonderful job of helping the child think about his audience, although she may not have thought of her actions in this way, and she certainly did not present the problem in a formal way to the child. The problem to be solved was a very practical one: A clear recipe needed to be formulated. It just so happened that the teacher was eliciting recipes from the children, and because of their inability to think of things from the point of view of others, recipes dictated often needed some rounding out, which is what the teacher helped the children do.

Teachers and parents might be able to think of a number of situations in which this kind of going over of a child's dictation might make sense. It would seem that this technique would work best when there is a real purpose for making the writing clearer. For example, a child who has dictated a story mostly for the pleasure of doing it should not be queried about possible missing details. If the story is for the child, there is no reason to try to think about another audience, anyway.

In addition, preschool children are just beginning to put their thoughts down, and this is enough of a task most of the time without being bothered about how the story would sound to someone else. We must use our good judgment here. On the other hand, if a child is dictating a thank you note for a gift, some assistance may be needed to help the child express pleasure about it in a way that will be understood by the recipient of the note.

Supporting children's writing efforts

The first and most important thing we can do to support children's beginning efforts at writing is to provide materials. A writ-

Subjects & Predicates

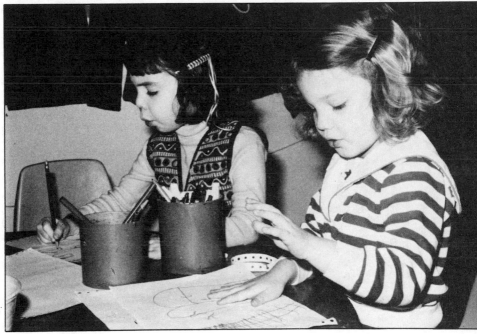

The first and most important thing we can do to support children's be-ginning efforts at writing is to provide materials: paper and various writing tools.

ing center, well supplied with paper and various writing tools, belongs in every preschool classroom. This is a place where children can experiment with and explore writing, and where they can go if they wish to write a message or create a story. Suggestions for organizing a writing center can be found in the next chapter. Parents, too, can make materials available to children at home, perhaps in an area near the grocery list or a desk where other family members routinely write letters or pay bills.

It is not our role to teach preschool children to write in the sense that we often think of teaching writing in the elementary school. Our role is to provide a print-rich environment (see the next chapter for suggestions), to answer children's questions, and to respond with interest and enthusiasm to children's writing creations.

There are times, of course, when questions intended to help a child think about her or his writing are appropriate and helpful.

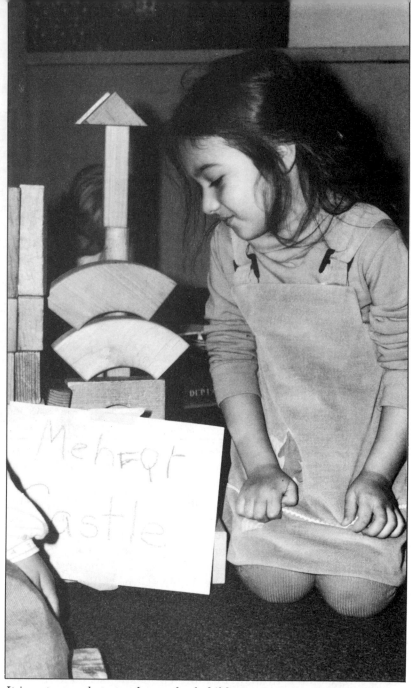

It is not our role to teach preschool children to write in the sense that we often think of teaching writing in the elementary school. Our role is to provide a print-rich environment, to answer children's questions, and to respond with interest and enthusiasm to children's writing creations.

The situation with the recipe is a good example of such an instance. But, by and large, we can facilitate children's writing development more during the preschool years if we do not develop any particular standard to which a child's writing should measure up. "Mistakes" are essential to the learning process, and as we saw earlier in this chapter, children apparently make mistakes deliberately in order to gain a better understanding of how to make letters, for example. While there are instances in which the characteristics of an error tell us that we can be helpful to a child's growth (for example, when Claire wrote her name as a mirror image), many errors are not of this kind and need no intervention from us.

To develop a helpful attitude toward children's writing behavior, teachers may find it useful to consider it in much the same way they consider children's behavior with art or blocks. We typically accept the ways children draw and build. We understand children's need to explore and experiment. A similar attitude of acceptance is appropriate at the writing center, too, although we tend to find it more difficult to overlook errors. It is especially hard to resist telling children how to do something. But children's writing requires the same kind of uncritical support, and we must give it generously.

References

Bissex, G. L. (1980). *GYNS AT WRK: A child learns to write and read.* Cambridge, MA: Harvard University Press.

Clay, M. (1975). *What did I write?* Portsmouth, NH: Heinemann.

Harste, J. C. (1983, February). *Preschoolers as writers.* Paper presented at the East-York-Scarborough Reading Association, Inc., conference, Toronto.

Harste, J. C., & Carey, R. F. (1979, October). Comprehension as setting. *Monographs in Language and Reading Series, 3,* 4–22.

Harste, J. C., Burke, C. L., & Woodward, V. A. (1981). *Children, their language and world: Initial encounters with print.* Final Report of the National Institute of Education Project # NIE-G-79-0132.

Holland, P. A. (1982). *Developing an awareness of written language.* Unpublished mimeo paper.

Lavine, L. (1977). Differentiation of letter-like forms in prereading children. *Developmental Psychology, 13*(2), 89–94.

Read, C. (1975). *Children's categorization of speech sounds in English.* Urbana, IL: National Council of Teachers of English.

Schickedanz, J. A., & Hultz, J. (1979). Unpublished data from the Boston University Preelementary Reading Improvement Project. (U.S. Office of Education Grant No. G007-605-403.)

Schickedanz, J. A., & Molina, A. (1979). Unpublished data from the Boston University Preelementary Reading Improvement Project. (U.S. Office of Education Grant No. G007-605-403.)

Schickedanz, J. A., & Sullivan, M. (1984, January). Mom, what does u-f-f spell? *Language Arts, 61*(1), 7–17.

Schickedanz, J. A., & Waldorf, B. (1980). Unpublished data from the Boston University Preelementary Reading Improvement Project. (U.S. Office of Education Grant No. G007-605-403.)

Selman, R. L. (1971). Taking another's perspective: Role taking development in early childhood. *Child Development, 42,* 1721–1734.

Whatever the activity or material, you can find possibilities to include print.

Chapter 5

Organizing the Environment To Support Literacy Development

When we create home and school environments for children, we choose the toys and materials we believe will both appeal to them and enhance their learning (NAEYC, 1985). Interestingly, we have traditionally excluded many literacy materials from the environment we create for young children.

For example, for dramatic play we include props such as dishes, dress-up clothes, dolls, and tables and chairs. But we have not usually included telephone books, magazines, or cookbooks; paper and pencils for writing notes; or books for reading stories to the dolls. When we enter children's play for brief periods to support or extend it, we burp the baby, eat pretend food, or ask for a hat. But rarely, if ever, do we say, *"Oh, I need to make a list before I go shopping,"* or *"I'm going to write a letter to Grandma."* But these literacy-related actions are as much a part of life as are the themes of cooking, bathing, or dressing up.

This chapter can help you create an environment in which literacy resources are provided to children, and in which literacy comes alive and is lived, both by adults and by children. It is organized by sections representing different types of literacy events. Parents can select and adapt some of these suggestions for use at home with preschool children.

Type of literacy event	Materials to support young children's literacy
Activities that help organize the environment and make life run smoothly	Labels Signs Charts Lists
Items commonly used during dramatic and other kinds of play	Print props—money, magazines, maps, containers Games Puzzles Cookbooks, recipe cards
Specific literacy skill materials	Alphabet materials, books Sound materials Word-making materials
Materials that support children's realistic literacy behavior	Book corner Writing center Writing suitcase

Organizing the environment

An early childhood classroom requires a certain degree of organization if it is to run smoothly. The physical environment must be arranged and kept in good order, and time must be scheduled. Labels, lists, signs, and charts can help us organize the environment and activities, and, in addition, provide functional print experiences for children.

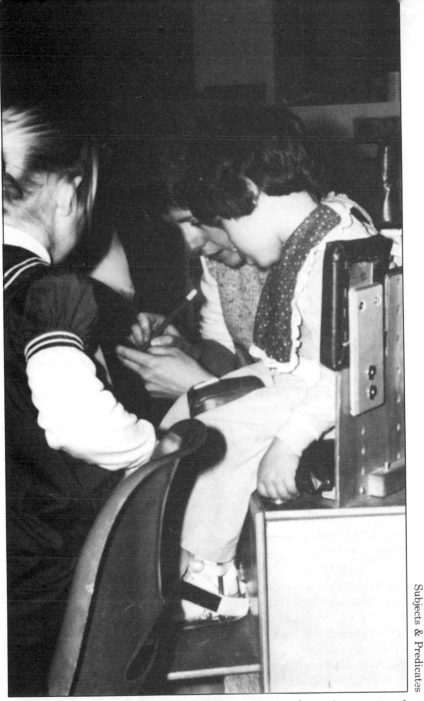

Labels, lists, signs, and charts can help us organize the environment and activities, and, in addition, provide functional print experiences for children.

Ask children to help prepare labels and attach them to containers and shelves.

Labels and signs

Every room for young children needs at least a few labels. For example, cubbies are labeled with children's names (using upper- and lower-case letters as appropriate) so that everyone knows whose cubby is whose. For younger children, a picture of an animal, in addition to a child's name, can be included on the cubby label to make identification of the space easier than it would be with the name alone.

Labels are also useful to indicate where in the room materials should be kept. If containers of materials belong in certain places on the shelves, both the containers and the shelves can be marked with matching labels. A picture of the item can be included on the labels, along with the print.

Children will need some assistance at first to learn that materials are to be returned to a specific shelf or place on a shelf, and that labels on the containers and shelves match. You can observe as children put things away and remind them to find the two labels that match. When children find the right spot for an item, you might comment: *"How wonderful. You found the place for the Attribute™ blocks. This label has pictures of Attribute™ blocks, and the words say 'Attribute™ blocks,' and so does this one."* Teachers also can model how materials are to be put away, by helping out at clean-up time. *"I'll put the markers away. Here's where they go. It says 'markers' right here."*

A good way to help children become aware of labels and their function is to ask them to help prepare the labels and attach them to containers and shelves. You might print the labels ahead of time and then ask children who are interested to help place them in the appropriate places. Children can decide where on a shelf various items might best be placed. Involvement of this kind in

Very little needs to be said about alphabetical order for children to gain an intuitive understanding of it.

arranging the materials and attaching labels helps children notice the labels and understand their purpose.

In addition to labels, many early childhood classrooms can put some signs or notices to good use. For example, a *Quiet please* sign might be placed in the library corner. A picture of a face with the letters *sh-sh-sh-sh* coming from the mouth might help children remember what the notice says.

Signs can also be useful if you wish to limit the number of children who may occupy an area in the classroom at any particular time. For example, it may be safe for only two children to work in the woodworking area. A notice that reads *Only two, please* could be posted, and a picture of two children could be pasted or drawn on the notice.

Many other signs may be of use, too. If routine directions are given in a particular place, a notice or sign might be considered. These can range from *Wash your hands, please,* and *Flush the toilet, please* signs in the bathroom, to *Walk, please* or *Watch your step, please* signs in a hallway or on the stairs.

As with labels, involvement in the creation of notices is likely to increase children's awareness of their content. When a sign seems to be needed, children who are interested can help make it.

Charts

Charts are lists or summaries of information, and these, too, can be used in preschool classrooms. For example, a helper's chart posts jobs that need to be done and the names of the children who are assigned to or volunteer for each job for the day or week. A helper's chart might look like the one in Figure 5.1.

Figure 5.1

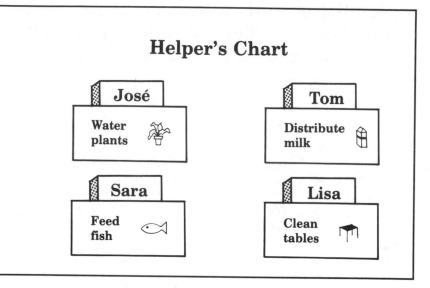

Helper's Chart

When tasks are assigned or selected on a daily, rather than a weekly, basis, children will have more opportunities to use the chart. You may be surprised at how quickly children learn to recognize their own names, as well as the names of their classmates, from a chart of this kind.

You may also wish to use an attendance chart. Young children often enjoy pocket charts like the one in Figure 5.2. When names are organized alphabetically, children have an opportunity to observe this type of organizational system. Children sometimes find it difficult to locate their name tags in a large assortment of tags. You may want to use a flat box lid to organize names by rows or first letter. Children soon learn what letter their name begins with and who else's name begins with that letter. They also gain an idea about whether their name starts with a letter that is near the beginning or the end of the alphabet. As with so many other things children learn, very little needs to be said about alphabetical order for children to gain an intuitive understanding of it. If you organize the attendance chart and the name tags in alphabetical order you have already said all that needs to be said.

Figure 5.2

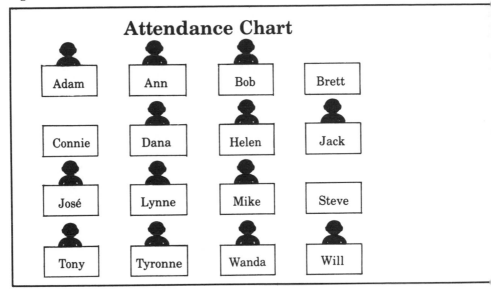

If children are to see any sense in maintaining the attendance chart each day, it must serve some useful purpose. For example, if cartons of milk need to be counted out for lunch or snack, this can be a job posted on the job chart. The children assigned to this task can count the number of name tags in the attendance chart pockets to see how many milk cartons are needed. For children who are just learning to count, the name tags can be taken out of the chart and placed on the tables. Children then can place a carton of milk at each place where there is a tag.

The attendance chart can be used in other ways, too. At group time, for example, you can help children determine who is absent. Children usually are interested in knowing if other children are sick or if they have gone on a trip. The specific reason for an absence can be discussed, if it is known. Such discussions also provide good opportunities for teachers to suggest that children may wish to write get-well cards to a child who is sick.

A third kind of chart which might be used is one on which the daily schedule is posted (Figure 5.3). When a child asks, *"When do we go outside?"* the teacher can refer to the chart as she or he

Figure 5.3

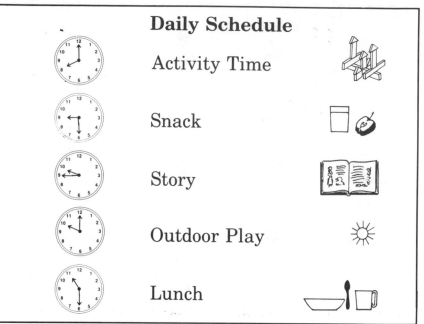

Daily Schedule

Activity Time

Snack

Story

Outdoor Play

Lunch

explains, *"First, we have snack, then we have story, and then we go outside."* Or, if a visitor or a new volunteer is in the classroom, children can be asked to review the daily schedule with them so they will know what the school day is like.

In addition to the daily schedule chart, a calendar can also be useful. All time concepts and instruments for measuring time are difficult for young children to comprehend. This is why it is important to relate to the child's own life and to represent time in ways that make sense to the child. A calendar used at group time to recite the day of the week, the date, the month, and the year has little meaning for young children.

When one group was asked what day it was, a 4-year-old responded, *"Payday!"* This response demonstrates how children can make a discussion about days more personally meaningful and related to their lives. A calendar on which children's birthdays are posted, or on which Halloween or other holidays are marked, or special activities indicated, takes on meaning. If calendars are

> If children are to see any sense in maintaining the attendance chart each day, it must serve some useful purpose.

used to help children see how many days it is until a birthday or a class field trip, then children can begin to appreciate a calendar's usefulness and to understand its structure.

If a calendar is designed so its parts (labels for days, weeks, months, and dates) are easily removed and rearranged, children can help create the calendar for each new month as it arrives. Pegboard and hooks can be used to create a versatile calendar. This activity itself can involve much learning. If the names of the months are stored in a box, a child can search in it to find the label for the particular month. The labels for the days of the week will stay in the same place, of course, but the numerals usually must be moved around to create the new month.

It is sometimes helpful to have children put the first few numerals up at the end of the last month to fill in the remaining days of the week. In this way, they can see why the first day of the next month may not fall on a Sunday, or the first day of the week. Children often want to begin the new month on the first day of the week. If you can help them see that the "old" month already used up those days, children begin to get the idea of how calendars work.

Special tags can be created to indicate special days. For example, a pumpkin tag may be created to hang on Halloween. Birthday cake tags with children's names written on them can indicate birthdays. These are then hung on the appropriate dates.

The important thing to remember about using a calendar with young children is that the primary objective is not for them to learn about the calendar. The primary objective is to give children a tool to understand the timing of events. In the process of using a calendar for this purpose, children will learn a lot about the structure of a calendar, probably much more than if days, months, and years are recited as a daily ritual.

107

The primary objective in using a calender with young children is to give them a tool to understand the timing of events.

You can find other good uses for the calendar, as well. For example, in programs where some children attend 1 or 3 days a week, while other children attend 5 days, some children's absences can be explained by reference to the calendar. *"Today is Tuesday. Jennifer comes only on Monday, Wednesday, and Friday. See, she'll be here tomorrow, because tomorrow is Wednesday. She's not sick today. This just isn't one of the days she comes to school."*

Or if it is Friday, you might refer to the calendar to explain that no one will come to school for 2 days. *"Tomorrow is Saturday and the next day is Sunday. We don't come to school on those days, do we? But we will be back on Monday."* The calendar also is helpful when you wish to explain to children that they will be away for several days for a vacation. If children can see the days, and perhaps count them, they can understand better just how long their teachers will be away.

Lists

Lists can also be used to support classroom organization. Suppose that a new activity or piece of equipment has been placed in the room. Chances are, many children will want a turn the first few days the new experience is available. One fair way to solve this problem of activity overload is to make a name list for turn-taking. In addition to solving the problem, this solution provides a good opportunity to demonstrate to children one of the main functions of written language: It helps us to keep track of, or to remember, things.

Children can participate most fully in using such lists by being invited to write their own names and by being referred to the name list when they ask, *"When will it be* my *turn?"* The teacher can say, *"Let's see. Helen is using the typewriter now. Then John gets a turn. Then Tyronne's name comes next, and your name follows his. It might be afternoon before you can have your turn. What else would you like to do while you wait? Tyronne will come to get you when it is your turn."* After children have taken their turns, they can cross their name off the list and see whose name appears next. You may need to help children read the next name, of course, especially if children have written their own names.

Other lists that children might routinely help devise include a shopping list for supplies for snack preparation, a list of favorite parts of a field trip, lists of steps to take when engaging in an activity or using a special piece of equipment, a list of items to take along on a walk, a list of foods to try—there are countless ways teachers and children can incorporate their planning and summarize meaningful events with the use of lists.

Summary

Many ideas for incorporating print into the classroom environment and routine situations have been suggested, and you can probably think of many others. These natural opportunities are some of the best ways to help children develop literacy knowledge because print used in these ways is meaningful and functional. In addition, the routine nature of these situations provides repeated encounters with print, which is important in helping children learn. Teachers are likely to marvel at the way children learn their own names and the names of classmates, and the content of signs and labels, just from being around these, day after day.

Incorporating print into dramatic play and other activities

Dramatic play

Aaron is sitting in the waiting room of the play doctor's office. The doctor is busy with a patient, so Aaron thumbs through a magazine.

Jessica runs from the play firestation with hose in hand, yelling *"Fire! Fire!"* Then she pauses, turns back toward the firestation, and says, *"I need my map."*

These two children, like most of their preschool peers, are deeply involved in dramatic play. But their behavior may be somewhat different—they are using props that contain print.

Play props. All of the common dramatic play themes—house, doctor's office, grocery store, fire station—can incorporate print props very naturally, for print props are an integral part of the real-life settings on which such play is based. Ideas for print props that might be included in typical dramatic play themes for young children are listed in Table 5.1.

Preparing for dramatic play. Play themes often emerge when they are prompted by a setting and props: Set up a house area, provide dishes, dolls, and dress-ups, and children typically engage in house play. Even within a theme, the type of props influence the plots played by the children: Dishes, kitchen appliances, and a table and chairs lead to cooking and eating. Dolls and doll clothes lead to parenting and dressing. Brooms, a dustpan, and empty cleaning containers lead to sweeping and dusting.

The number of props can also influence the complexity of play. For example, a dish cloth, a scouring pad, an empty dish detergent bottle, a dish rack, and a dish towel are likely to result in more varied dishwashing behaviors than would occur if only dishes and a sink were provided.

One way to provide for satisfying and engaging dramatic play is to start with a skeleton setup and then add props gradually to keep the play area interesting. Many print props will be appreciated more and used more fully if they are added a few at a time, or in response to children's spontaneous actions. For example, the teacher might notice in house play that a child pretended there was a fire and called the fire station. An emergency number decal to attach to the phone might be particularly appreciated on the following day. Or, if the teacher has noticed that shopping trips have become a popular plot in house play, the addition of note pads and pencils may be just the thing to keep interest going.

New props can be placed in a play area for children to discover, without comment from the teacher, or the teacher can explain what she or he had in mind. *"I thought you might like these note pads to make lists for your shopping trips."* Whatever the method of introduction, children are likely to use any prop in a number of ingenious ways. These innovations must be respected as long as they make a positive contribution to the play.

All of the common dramatic play themes can incorporate print props very naturally, for print props are an integral part of the real-life settings on which such play is based.

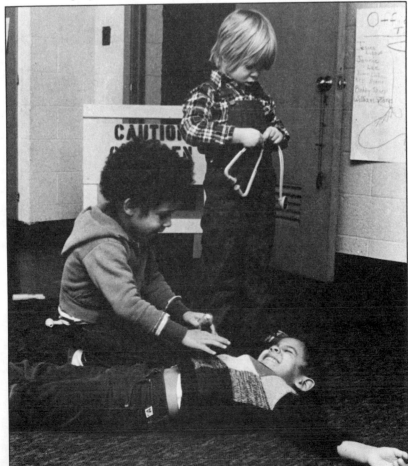

Bruce Jennings

Table 5.1.

Print props to add to children's dramatic play.

House play

Books to read to dolls or stuffed animals.
Empty food, toiletry, and cleaning containers.
Telephone books. (Make them with children's names, addresses, and telephone numbers. Cover pages with clear plastic adhesive.)
Emergency numbers decal to attach to the play phone. Write in numbers for doctor, ambulance, fire station, and police.
Cookbook. (Can be made with children's favorite recipes.)
Small notepads and a container with pencils.
Wall plaques with appropriate verses.
Stationery and envelopes.
Magazines and newspapers.
Food coupons.
Grocery store food ads.
Play money.

Doctor's office play

Eye chart posted on the wall. (Make one with rows of different size letters.)
Telephone book.
Message pad and pencils.
Signs such as *Doctor is in/Doctor is out, Thank you for not smoking, Open/Closed.*
Magazines and books for the waiting room.
Pamphlets for children about health care (brushing teeth, eating good foods, wearing safety belts).
File folders and ditto sheets for health charts.
Index cards cut in quarters for appointment cards.

Grocery store play

Empty food containers.
Labels for store departments: dairy, produce, etc.
Food posters. (Ask a supermarket for old ones.)

Brown grocery bags with the name of the store written on them.
Signs for store hours.
Numeral stamps and stamp pads to price foods.
Play money, cash register.
Grocery store ads.

Restaurant play

Menus.
Magnetic letters and board to post specials.
Placemats. (Cover construction paper with the name of the restaurant written on it in clear plastic adhesive.)
Note pads and pencils for taking orders and writing checks.
Play money, cash register.
Open and closed signs.

Transportation play

Recipe cards cut in half for tickets.
Maps or an atlas.
Suitcases with luggage tags.
Travel brochures.
Little notebooks for record keeping.

Post office play

Envelopes of various sizes.
Stationery supplies, pencils.
Stickers or gummed stamps.
Stamp pad and stamp to cancel.

Office play

Typewriter or computer terminal and paper.
Telephone book.
Ledger sheets.
Dictation pads, other note pads.
3-ring binders filled with information.
Sales brochures.
Business cards made from file cards.
Filing supplies.
Date and other stamps and stamp pad.

Start with a skeleton setup and then add props gradually to keep the dramatic play area interesting.

Guiding the play. We must not distort children's dramatic play in order to teach any specific skills. Children will learn simply by using various props in their play. However, when children invite us to play, or when we think that joining their play for a brief period would support their goals, we have a chance, through example, to demonstrate knowledge to children. For example, if we are invited to be the patient in the doctor's office play, we can ask for an appointment card before leaving the office. Or, if children are having difficulty organizing their play because of their limited knowledge of the roles people play in various settings, we can help out: *"I see you have an overflow of patients today, doctor. I'll be the receptionist and find magazines for people to read in the waiting room until you are ready to see them."* As the receptionist, you might organize an appointment book and make out appointment cards for departing patients.

Adults who are sensitive partners in children's play never stay involved for long, unless children truly need them to fill a role that sustains the play. While playing, we must allow children to take the lead in directing the play. The play must fulfill the children's purposes, not our preconceived notions of what we think should be taught.

In addition to guiding the play through participation, we can influence play less directly. Books about various occupations and jobs can be placed in the class library. Visitors can be invited to talk about their jobs and to show children special tools they use in their work. Trips can be taken so children can see firsthand what various people do. Teachers can make a special effort to help visitors bring along print-related props. For example, a nurse often brings along a stethoscope, an otoscope, and a tongue depressor, but can also be asked to bring a health or vision chart.

We must not distort children's dramatic play in order to teach any specific skills. Children will learn simply by using various props in their play.

When children take trips, you can point out print-related activities, along with the more obvious tasks and equipment that teachers and children often notice. Of course, thank you notes must be sent to visitors or to hosts for trips—a wonderful opportunity for children to develop literacy skills.

Other activities

Print can be included in many activities for young children. For example, miniature road signs can be included in the block area. Index cards, scissors, markers, and tape might also be available if children wish to create signs for buildings or for animal cages in a zoo, for example. In addition, some of the play people figures often have print on them. One set of women workers has *bus* written on a bus one of them drives, and *U.S. Mail* on the mail bag. Some vehicles intended for use with blocks also have words printed on them. The same props, or similar ones, can be included in sand play when children are building roads, cities, or zoos.

Puzzles, too, can be selected for their print potential. Puzzles with road signs always contain print, and some occupation puzzles have labels such as *school crossing guard* or *police officer.* Some storybook puzzles contain the titles of the nursery rhyme or story.

Picture lotto games often have the name of the object underneath the picture. Certainly picture lotto games you make can easily have this added feature.

Sometimes manipulative math materials include numeral cards to match with sets of objects. And sometimes the numeral name is spelled out on the cards, beneath the Arabic numeral. When you make such materials, you can include the words for the numeral. You might also include the name of any sets of objects pictured, such as *3 kittens.*

Whatever the activity or material, you can find possibilities to include print. Many activities will be enhanced by print in the form of labels and signs as we discussed earlier. Plants grown in a science area might be labeled *marigolds, beans, coleus.* Or a sign could be made for a fish tank to give the names of the fish. Such a sign could even be in the form of an activity card:

Can you find the *catfish?*
Can you find the *snails?*
Can you find the *guppies?*

A magnifying glass near the fish tank will encourage children to search. Pictures of each animal, perhaps cut out from a magazine and pasted on the activity card, will help the children know what they are looking for.

When children cook, use a recipe chart. These large attractive displays of the recipe make it easy for children to follow along.

Using books in conjunction with various classroom activities is also an important way to nurture children's literacy development. When children need to decide what kind of guinea pig to buy or what to feed it, a book can be consulted. Or when children wonder what kind of leaves have just blown in the school yard, why a cut finger bleeds, or what kinds of seeds certain birds like to eat, they can find answers in books.

Some of the books children need may not be in the classroom, but among your own resources instead. Others will be in the school or city library. Wherever the needed book might be, by helping children find information in books, you are teaching children about the value of print in everyday life.

Literacy materials designed for children

Two children are playing with a deck of labeled picture cards. Each draws one card from the deck, then turns it face up on the table. Suddenly, after the fourth or fifth round of turns, one child announces, *"I have a pair! I have a pair! 'Key' and 'pea' rhyme!"* He places these cards together, then sets them apart from the others on the table. The game continues.

In another area of the room, a child quickly finishes placing all of the alphabet letters back in the wooden puzzle frame from which they had been dumped. And yet another child tries to keep his balance as he walks the narrow curved line forming one loop of a giant letter *B* that has been placed on the floor of the active play area with masking tape.

In all of these situations, children are learning more than literacy skills; social skills, spatial skills, and motor skills are being enhanced as well. But we might say that the materials have a specific intent to facilitate the development of literacy skills and that their designers were especially sensitive to the ways in which preschoolers can best be engaged in learning. Unlike the activities in the last section, where the print was added to support and enrich other goals, the materials and activities to be discussed here have literacy development as a more primary goal.

Specific literacy materials often isolate various skills from the context of complete and meaningful written language.

Are specific materials needed to facilitate literacy development?

If this chapter had ended with the last section, we could feel fairly secure that children's literacy development would proceed very well indeed. In fact, the most important ways to support literacy development have already been discussed. This is because written language is kept **whole** and functional and meaningful when used in the ways already noted. This wholeness allows children to use all of their current knowledge in their efforts to understand written language.

Specific literacy materials often isolate various skills from the context of complete and meaningful written language—sounds and letters are isolated from whole words, handwriting is isolated from conveying a message, writing a story is separated from gaining an appreciation for an audience, reading words is separated from reading text. Separation and isolation of such skills can make written language learning into a very great mystery for children and can severely limit children's ability and desire to learn. Worse yet, if only a few isolated skills are stressed, children are prevented from gaining a complete understanding of the total reading and writing process. So, specific literacy materials can lead to problems.

But if specific literacy materials are kept in proper perspective, and are kept in their place as simply a very small part of a total literacy development plan, they can add to children's learning. There are times when children may wish to practice skills in isolation. Perhaps a child has been singing a song for several months and has just begun to appreciate the fact that it contains rhyming words. This child might now enjoy playing with the deck of cards that contains pairs of labeled pictures whose names rhyme. And depending on the child's other skills, you may wish to point out the similarities in the spellings of the names of the rhyming pairs the child finds.

Literacy skill play must take place within a larger context of meaningful written language.

Susan May

Or perhaps children have noticed print in the environment and in books, and have been interested in the letters of their names. Such children may truly enjoy long periods of play with a set of magnetic alphabet letters, searching for familiar letters, comparing letters, and placing letters they think are alike in groups.

The important thing is to remember that literacy skill play must take place within a larger context of meaningful written language. While the child may *physically* be isolated from this larger context at certain times, no psychological isolation need exist—children bring the larger context, gained from experience, to any episode of isolated skill play; and they take back to whole experiences any new insights gained from skill play. When we allow children to choose when and if they will use skill materials, we can be fairly certain they will be used with some understanding of their place in the larger context of whole language.

Literacy skills materials for young children

Alphabet materials. Alphabet materials come in many styles and forms. Several distinctly different sets are probably worth having. You may wish to select an alphabet puzzle, a set of both upper- and lower-case magnetic letters, an attractive alphabet chart to post on the wall, and, perhaps, small, 1-inch cubes with letters on their sides. In addition, alphabet lotto or bingo games, which are easy to make, are probably worth including. And, of course, several attractive and interesting alphabet books can be included in the library corner, along with the other books.

Sound materials. This category includes materials that stress rhyming words, as well as those that ask children to select words on the basis of similar consonant sounds either at the beginning or end of the word. There are many commercial materials of this kind. They usually contain several pairs of pictures whose names rhyme, or whose beginning or ending sounds are the same. A deck containing pictures of a cake and a rake, a house and a mouse, and a bat and a hat are typical of the former, whereas decks containing pictures of a ball and a bat, a cat and a car, and a dog and a duck are characteristic of the latter. Sets that have the picture label printed on them may be more useful than sets with pictures alone, for as Chapter 3 notes, exposure to print may facilitate a child's ability to think about oral language in terms of individual phonemes.

Many variations of these basic materials can be devised. For example, you might divide a piece of construction paper into four or six sections and then label each section with a letter. Then prepare a deck of picture cards so that there are several whose names begin with each of the letters appearing in the section on the construction paper. Children go through the deck and sort the pictures.

The reader can, no doubt, imagine many more variations on these basic themes. Homemade materials will last longer, of course, if they are laminated or covered with clear adhesive paper.

Word-making materials. These may be sets of alphabet letters that are specially designed. The individual pieces are typically smaller than other alphabet sets, and all letters (especially the common vowels) are available in multiples. The letters from a Scrabble™ game serve nicely here, and there are other commerical materials of this kind in both wood and plastic. You can make your own set, of course, with tagboard.

Other word-making materials are more structured and restricted in their design and use. For example, flip cards that leave the root of a word the same, while the intial letter changes, are common. Thus a word might change from bat, to cat, to rat, to mat. Dial-a-word and turn-a-word materials are similar, although their pieces turn, rather than flip. Any comprehensive early childhood materials catalog will have a wide variety of these more limited activities.

Materials to support children's realistic literacy behavior

As we have seen, young children like to read books and write letters or stories. Their efforts can best be supported with a book corner and a writing center, both permanent features in the classroom.

The book corner

Because we discussed the book corner in Chapter 3, we will add only a few more ideas here. Variety of books, some of which are

---

Visit the writing center to offer encouragement and help to the children, and to do some writing yourself.

---

predictable, is clearly important. It is also an advantage for children that at least some of the books remain in the area for a very long period of time, perhaps several months. Children need time with a book to learn the story well and to experiment in matching speech to print. Books from a public library certainly can augment a classroom book corner, but children need other books that can remain in their book corner longer than the typical 3-week library loan period allows.

While children enjoy new stories, they enjoy hearing old favorites, too. Teachers who join children in the book corner should not be surprised, or dismayed, when children request to have the same stories read over and over again. Teachers may want to read one new story during group storytime each day, and then follow it with a favorite and familiar story for the classroom book corner. The library books to which the children respond most favorably may be the ones you will want to purchase for the classroom book corner. Then these will become the new old favorites, as time goes on.

The writing center

Because children often wish to make greeting cards or books; write notes, letters, or stories; or experiment with various writing materials, they need a place in the classroom for these activities. This area, like the literacy skills materials area discussed earlier, need not be large. Because it will be available every day during the activity period, when children may choose between it and many other centers, space for three or four children to work comfortably will be adequate. A table and several chairs, plus a shelf for storing writing materials, will provide the basic setup for the area. Writing supplies will vary, but might include a selection of items such as those listed in Table 5.2.

Table 5.2.

Writing supplies for the writing center.

Pencils. (Thin lead with eraser. Thick lead without eraser. Colored pencils. Wax pencils if appropriate surfaces are available.)

Markers. (Both wide- and fine-tipped, available in a variety of colors, all watercolor.)

Magic slates and wooden pencils.

Alphabet letter stamps and ink pads.

Typewriter or computer with word processing.

Paper. (Plain newsprint, white and colored construction paper, typing or mimeo paper, computer print-out paper, carbon paper.)

Acetate sheets and wipe-off cloths.

Letter and design stencils.

Index and computer cards.

Stapler.

Hole punch.

Scissors.

Paste and glue.

Pencil sharpener.

Book of wallpaper samples for use as book covers.

Stationery, perhaps created with stickers.

Envelopes.

Old magazines.

Chalk and chalkboard.

Bits of string and yarn.

Children will be attracted to the writing center if it is appealing, if materials are kept in good working order (no dried-out markers), and if you visit the center to offer encouragement and help to the children and to do some writing yourself from time to time.

There is no need to set aside time to teach formal lessons to young children about reading and writing. Children will learn about written language because it is part of their lives.

You can also make suggestions for writing that needs to be done. For example, if a sample of the bread the children baked is sent to the school receptionist, a note that expresses the children's appreciation for the receptionist's services can be made and sent along. Welcome-back signs or get-well greetings can be made for children or adults who are away from school for a period of time.

Such tasks must not be made in the form of assignments. In fact, you might announce that you are going to be working on such an item and suggest that anyone who is interested may help. Chances are, children will want to help. Once begun, you can offer to let the children assume more responsibility for the activity.

> When *children,* and not *teaching children,* are the focus, meaningful learning takes place.

Another intriguing idea is to prepare a writing suitcase (Rich, 1985) for children to take home on weekends or evenings. Some of the same items found in the writing center can be selected to put in a portable resource kit.

Summary

As we have seen throughout this book, there are many ways to surround young children with print and to engage them in literacy activities. When parents and teachers plan children's environments and activities carefully so that literacy is an integral part of everything they do, then literacy learning becomes a natural and meaningful part of children's everyday lives. When you create this kind of environment, there is no need to set aside time to teach formal lessons to children about reading and writing. Children will learn about written language because it is part of their life.

And it is the life of the classroom that must be your focus. What are children's goals? What do they try to do? What problems get in their way? What do they not understand? What are they feeling? Written language is a tool that can help children do things: A note posted on a block building can alert others that it is to stay up until tomorrow. A calendar can help a child understand how many days it is until his mother returns from a business trip. Paper and pencil in the dramatic play area can enrich the way children choose to play father, mother, or doctor. Labels and signs can help children know where to find things and to remember how to behave in certain areas. And a note to mom or dad, which says in scribble, *"I miss you,"* can help ease the loneliness that children sometimes feel when they are separated from their parents all day long, and can help them greet a parent positively instead of with ambivalence or anger upon reunion. A list of suggested names for the new rabbit can be compiled, and children can vote for their choice. When *children,* and not *teaching children,* are the focus, meaningful learning takes place.

References

NAEYC. (1985). (NAEYC# 571). Toys: Tools for learning. Washington, DC: Author.

Rich, S. J. (1985, July). The writing suitcase. *Young Children, 40*(5), 42–44.

Appendix 1

Helping Children Learn About Reading

A word to parents

Parents often think that children learn about reading in elementary school. The truth of the matter is that many children already know a lot about reading when they enter kindergarten because parents have been teaching their children about reading from the time the children were born.

The methods parents use to teach children reading differ from those typically used in elementary school. Parents help children learn about reading every day—when they take them to the grocery store or when they point out street signs, for example. This kind of experience with print gives children a broad and meaningful introduction to reading. Reading really cannot be learned very well if we start only with lessons on isolated letters and sounds. If reading is to make sense to children, they must see how it is used in life.

Think how silly it would be to give a baby talking lessons, to make sounds out of context and then expect the baby to repeat these! The baby might learn to make sounds and say words, but might never learn to use words to communicate with others. While children enjoy playing with language, they need much more to learn how to read.

Children who become good readers are those who have had many experiences with print during their early years. They probably have seen their parents reading for pleasure or to obtain information. Reading becomes a part of their lives long before elementary school. Even after children enter elementary school, families can provide a variety of experiences that will help children make the best of their activities in a larger group. Although schools may have capable and dedicated teachers, schools are by their nature isolated from the larger world. Children learn from everything they see and do—at home, at school, and everywhere else. Here are some ideas for families who want to help their children learn about reading.

How parents can help

Infants. Talk to your baby—during bathtime, at play, when changing clothes or a diaper, at feeding times. Language is the cornerstone of reading development.

Sing to your baby—children's songs or anything that you enjoy.

Prop up a cardboard book for the 2- to 4-month-old baby in the crib or on the floor. Select books with simple, bright pictures.

Read or recite nursery rhymes to your baby.

Babies from 6 to 12 months will look at, chew, pound on, or toss books. Cardboard or cloth books can be part of a child's toy selection. Paper books can be reserved for lap reading times.

Name and point to the pictures in books when your baby seems interested.

After you have been naming pictures for a few weeks, begin to ask "Where's the teddy bear?" Soon your baby will bat at or put a finger on the picture of the teddy bear.

Babies can ask "What is that?" by pointing to pictures and babbling. This question-and-answer game is fun and helps increase your baby's vocabulary.

Before the age of 1 year, most babies like to handle books more than they like to listen to you read. Your baby's behavior will make it clear which is more interesting at the time.

Babies who laugh and smile when you play Pat-a-Cake, Peek-a-Boo, or This Little Piggy are old enough to play these games.

When your baby is old enough to sit up easily in a grocery cart, give her or him small unbreakable items to hold, such as a little box of raisins or crackers. Talk with your baby about the box and what is inside.

If you go to a restaurant that uses paper placemats, point out the pictures on the placemat. Babies also enjoy holding plastic-covered menus.

Take your baby to the park, the zoo, the library, the store. Babies learn from everything they see.

Babies can sit on your lap, in an infant seat, or in a high chair while you write letters or make grocery lists. Talk to your baby about what you are doing. Offer toys to younger babies. Children from about age 1 can begin to use blunt writing instruments such as watercolor markers to write on their own paper.

Junk mail is ideal reading material for your baby while you read the other mail. Just make sure baby doesn't eat the mail!

At about 1 year of age children may begin to notice the letters on wooden blocks or other toys. Talk about the letters or words and what they mean.

Toddlers. Toddlers will continue to ask questions about pictures or print. You can help your toddler make the transition from "Dat?" or "Whassat?" to "What's that?" by repeating "What's that?" before answering the question.

Stories can be used occasionally to help a child make a transition between active play and more restful activities. Reading books at bedtime has been a favorite of children for generations.

Toddlers who have been read to since babyhood sometimes ask you to read their favorites repeatedly. Sometimes you may want to encourage your toddler to read the book alone while you are close by to comment. Other times when you read together you may want to pause before a familiar word to give your child a chance to point to the picture or say the missing word. Rhyming books are a good way to introduce this game.

Toddlers love to write and draw. Shelf paper or discarded computer paper makes inexpensive large sheets. Offer wide- and thin-tipped watercolor markers to your child. Establish a place for drawing to help your toddler understand that walls are not for drawing on. Drawing materials should be kept out of the toddler's reach, but offered often.

Children enjoy sticking magnetic letters on the refrigerator. Soon you can spell the child's name, or the names of other family members. You can name the letters as you would any other object. Sometimes, just for fun, make your child's name and leave a few other letters as well. Ask your child to find her or his name. Increase the number of extra letters as the toddler's skills grow.

Take your child to the library or bookstore to choose books. Some libraries have story hours for toddlers.

Continue to encourage your child to write shopping lists with you. Give your child coupons for a few favorite grocery items, and ask her or him to show you the coupon for a specific item.

Expand your child's horizons by taking short trips to interesting new places—a street festival, a sheep-shearing—and talk about what is happening. Read posters or programs for the event. Before you go, prepare your child by discussing what you will do. Read about similar functions if possible.

Letters or thank you notes drawn by toddlers may be treasured by friends and relatives. Be sure to read letters aloud when they arrive from others.

Preschoolers. Your child is probably saying familiar stories along with you by now, or perhaps insists on reading to you sometimes. If you are reading and skip a word, you will surely be corrected. This is an extremely important step in learning about reading. Add some new books to your child's collection, of course, but keep reading old favorites.

At this age, shopping is still a marvelous way to help your child see how print works. Preschoolers can select items from the shelf. Cooking together is a terrific way to demonstrate how reading can be used to follow a recipe. Children can assemble the ingredients, stir, and pour while you read the directions.

When eating out, read napkins, placemats, and other printed items with your child. Some of the games printed on placemats are for older children, but younger ones may enjoy drawing on the paper.

Take books with you on long rides or for times when you must wait quietly.

Play games such as *Go Fish, Hi-Ho! Cherry-O,* or picture dominoes. Read the directions aloud and point out print on the materials. Don't expect preschoolers to play games perfectly—they have different ideas about what it means to follow rules.

Children ages 4 or 5 may begin to ask about print in books. You also might want to call attention to the print by asking questions such as "Where does it say *Max* on the boat?" Books with labeled pictures make it possible for children to use their knowledge of pictures to read the words.

Help your child make greeting cards. Older children might want to copy some words, or may ask for spellings. Give one letter at a time. Now writing materials can be made freely accessible to children. Typewriters or home computers might also be a way to encourage emerging writing skills.

Use magnetic or wooden letters to spell important words for your child. You might make a few cards with these words written on them so that the child can select letters to form the words.

School-age children. Continue to read to and with your child, especially at bedtime, even if your child has learned to read. You can read one page and then your child can read one page.

Regular stops at the library are still important. Many libraries issue cards to children who can write their own names.

Control the amount of TV that the family watches. Have a family quiet hour every night for reading, writing, or doing homework.

Purchase stationery or paper, pens, and stickers for making stationery so your child can write thank you notes or greeting cards.

Encourage story writing by listening to the stories your child writes. Typewriters or home computers are excellent helps for story writing.

Join in when your child tells jokes or riddles. Language play helps your child think about sounds, words, and meanings.

Play word games such as *Scrabble* or *Boggle* with your child. Purchase inexpensive books of crossword puzzles and other word games that are convenient for taking in the car.

Books for parents

Butler, D. (1982). *Babies need books.* New York: Atheneum. Lots of good
ideas and some strong opinions about how and what to read to very
young children.

Butler, D. (1979). *Cushla and her books.* Boston: Horn Book. A case study
of a handicapped child and how books played an important role from
infancy.

Butler, D., & Clay, M. (1979). *Reading begins at home.* Exeter, NH:
Heinemann. Gives sensible information about what reading really is.
Provides many ideas for parents.

Chall, J. S. (1983). *Stages of reading development.* New York: McGraw
Hill. Gives a thorough description of each stage a child goes through
in learning to read. Differentiates prereading from initial reading stage.

Clay, M. (1987). *Writing begins at home.* Portsmouth, NH: Heinemann.

Larrick, N. (1982). *A parent's guide to children's reading* (5th ed.).
New York: Bantam Books. Good lists of books for children.

Rossi, M. J. M. (1982). *Read to me: Teach me.* Wauwatosa, WI:
American Baby Books. Good descriptions of many books for children from
birth to age 5.

Schickedanz, J. (1990). *Adam's righting revolutions: A case study of
writing development from age one to age seven.* Portsmouth, NH:
Heinemann.

Books for children

These are some of the *many* good books for young children. The
children's librarian can help you find others of interest to your
child.

2 to 6 months.

Baby's First Golden Book Series. Milne, A. A. (1977). *Little animal friends,
What does baby see?, Play with me,* and *Winnie the Pooh's rhymes.*
Racine, WI: Western Publishing. A set of four books with content related to a baby's life: animals, toys, games, and rhymes. Plastic coated
paper that can be mouthed.

Bruna, D. (1980). *My toys.* New York: Methuen. A zigzag book. Good for
propping up and naming pictures.

Chorao, K. (1977). *The baby's lap book.* New York: Dutton. Rhymes and
verses to read while baby is in your lap.

Looking at animals. (1981). Los Angeles: Price, Stern & Sloan. Stiff cardboard and colorful. Good for looking at and naming pictures.

6 to 12 months. All those listed above and these:

Baby's first book. (1960). New York: Platt & Munk. Stiff cardboard pages with many familiar objects to name.

Bruna, D. (1967). *B is for bear.* New York: Methuen. A colorful alphabet book.

Gillham, B. (1982). *The first words picture book.* New York: Coward, McCann, & Geoghegan. Color photographs of familiar objects. Paper pages.

Miller, J. P. (1979). *The cow says moo.* New York: Random House. A cloth book with farm animals and their sounds.

My house. (1978). New York: Golden. Stiff cardboard book with colorful pictures of everyday things. Rounded corners make it safe for the beginning sitter.

Sesame Street. Ernie and Bert can . . . can you? (1982). New York: Random House. A little Chubby Book with cardboard pages that spring up to ease page turning.

12 to 24 months.

Brown, M. W. (1975). *Goodnight moon.* New York: Harper & Row. Lovely simple story in which many things are told goodnight.

Burningham, J. (1975). *The blanket.* New York: Crowell. A little boy can't find his blanket so everyone looks for it.

Freeman, D. (1968). *Corduroy.* New York: Penguin. Your child may not yet have enough patience to listen to the story, but many toddlers love to find Corduroy on each page.

Fujikawa, G. (1975). *Baby animals.* New York: Grosset & Dunlap. A lovely stiff cardboard book with simple text and charming pictures.

Scarry, R. (1980). *Best word book ever.* New York: Golden. A book virtually filled with pictures to name and talk about.

2 to 3 years.

Carle, E. (1972). *The very hungry caterpillar.* New York: Philomel. A tiny caterpillar grows fat from eating all kinds of things. The repetitive and predictable verse and delightful illustrations will charm children.

Keats, E. J. (1962). *The snowy day.* New York: Penguin. Children will identify with Peter who has fun playing in the snow.

Spier, P. (1971). *Gobble, growl, grunt.* New York: Doubleday. Pictures of dozens of animals and their sounds.

3 to 5 years. These plus the 2 to 3 years list.

Heller, R. (1981). *Chickens aren't the only ones*. New York: Grosset & Dunlap. A *beautiful* book about animals who lay eggs. Informative and delightful.

Kredenser, G., & Mack, S. (1971). *One dancing drum*. New York: S. G. Phillips. A counting book with wonderful alliteration and 10 interesting instruments.

McCloskey, R. (1948). *Blueberries for Sal*. New York: Viking. Also, (1982). New York: Penguin, Picture Puffins. A little bear and a little girl mix up their mothers while gathering blueberries.

Wildsmith, B. (1962). *Brian Wildsmith's ABC*. New York: Franklin Watts. Beautifully illustrated, as are all of Wildsmith's books.

Copies of "Helping Children Learn About Reading," by Judith Schickedanz, are available from NAEYC in the form of a brochure. 50¢ each; 100 for $10

National Association for
  the Education of Young Children
1509 16th Street, N.W.
Washington, DC 20036-1426
202-232-8777 800-424-2460

Appendix 2

A Joint Statement of Concerns about Present Practices in Pre-First Grade Reading Instruction and Recommendations for Improvement

- Association for Supervision and Curriculum Development
- International Reading Association
- National Association for the Education of Young Children
- National Association of Elementary School Principals
- National Council of Teachers of English
- Association for Childhood Education International

Prepared by the Early Childhood and Literacy Development Committee of the International Reading Association

Objectives for a pre-first grade reading program

Literacy learning begins in infancy. Reading and writing experiences at school should permit children to build upon their already existing knowledge of oral and written language. Learning should take place in a supportive environment where children can build a positive attitude toward themselves and toward language and literacy. For optimal learning, teachers should involve children actively in many meaningful, functional language experiences, including *speaking, listening, writing,* and *reading.* Teachers of young children should be prepared in ways that acknowledge differences in language and cultural backgrounds and emphasize reading as an integral part of the language arts as well as of the total curriculum.

What young children know about oral and written language before they come to school

1. Children have had many experiences from which they are building their ideas about the functions and uses of oral language and written language.

2. Children have a command of language, have internalized many of its rules, and have conceptualized processes for learning and using language.

3. Many children can differentiate between drawing and writing.

4. Many children are reading environmental print, such as road signs, grocery labels, and fast food signs.

5. Many children associate books with reading.

6. Children's knowledge about language and communication systems is influenced by their social and cultural backgrounds.

7. Many children expect that reading and writing will be sense-making activities.

Concerns

1. Many pre-first grade children are subjected to rigid, formal pre-reading programs with inappropriate expectations and experiences for their levels of development.

2. Little attention is given to individual development or individual learning styles.

3. The pressures of accelerated programs do not allow children to be risk-takers as they experiment with language and internalize concepts about how language operates.

4. Too much attention is focused upon isolated skill development or abstract parts of the reading process, rather than upon the integration of oral language, writing, and listening with reading.

5. Too little attention is placed upon reading for pleasure; therefore, children often do not associate reading with enjoyment.

6. Decisions related to reading programs are often based on political and economic considerations rather than on knowledge of how young children learn.

7. The pressure to achieve high scores on standardized tests that frequently are not appropriate for the kindergarten child has resulted in changes in the content of programs. Program content often does not attend to the child's social, emotional, and intellectual development. Consequently, inappropriate activities that deny curiosity, critical thinking, and creative expression occur all too frequently. Such activities foster negative attitudes toward communication skill activities.

8. As a result of declining enrollments and reduction in staff, individuals who have little or no knowledge of early childhood education are sometimes assigned to teach young children. Such teachers often select inappropriate methodologies.

9. Teachers of pre-first graders who are conducting individualized programs without depending upon commercial readers and workbooks need to articulate for parents and other members of the public what they are doing and why.

Recommendations

1. Build instruction on what the child already knows about oral language, reading, and writing. Focus on meaningful experiences and meaningful language rather than merely on isolated skill development.

2. Respect the language the child brings to school, and use it as a base for language and literacy activities.

3. Ensure feelings of success for all children, helping them see themselves as people who can enjoy exploring oral and written language.

4. Provide reading experiences as an integrated part of the broader communication process, which includes speaking, listening, and writing, as well as other communication systems such as art, math, and music.

5. Encourage children's first attempts at writing without concern for the proper formation of letters or correct conventional spelling.

6. Encourage risk-taking in first attempts at reading and writing and accept what appear to be errors as part of children's natural patterns of growth and development.

7. Use materials for instruction that are familiar, such as well-known stories, because they provide the child with a sense of control and confidence.

8. Present a model for students to emulate. In the classroom, teachers should use language appropriately, listen and respond to children's talk, and engage in their own reading and writing.

9. Take time regularly to read to children from a wide variety of poetry, fiction, and non-fiction.

10. Provide time regularly for children's independent reading and writing.

11. Foster children's affective and cognitive development by providing opportunities to communicate what they know, think, and feel.

12. Use evaluative procedures that are developmentally and culturally appropriate for the children being assessed. The selection of evaluative measures should be based on the objectives of the instructional program and should consider each child's total development and its effect on reading performance.

13. Make parents aware of the reasons for a total language program at school and provide them with ideas for activities to carry out at home.

14. Alert parents to the limitations of formal assessments and standardized tests of pre-first graders' reading and writing skills.

15. Encourage children to be active participants in the learning process rather than passive recipients of knowledge by using activities that allow for experimentation with talking, listening, writing, and reading.

"Literacy Development and Pre-First Grade" is available as a brochure from the International Reading Association. Single copies are free with a self-addressed, stamped envelope. The brochure is also available in quantities of 100 for $8, prepaid only. Write International Reading Association, 800 Barksdale Rd., P.O. Box 8139, Newark, DE 19714-8139.

Index

Information about NAEYC

NAEYC IS...

... a membership-supported organization of people committed to fostering the growth and development of children from birth through age 8. Membership is open to all who share a desire to serve and act on behalf of the needs and rights of young children.

NAEYC PROVIDES...

... educational services and resources to adults who work with and for children, including

• *Young Children, the* journal for early childhood educators

• **Books, posters, brochures,** and **videos** to expand your knowledge and commitment to young children, with topics including infants, curriculum, research, discipline, teacher education, and parent involvement

• An **Annual Conference** that brings people from all over the country to share their expertise and advocate on behalf of children and families

• **Week of the Young Child** celebrations sponsored by NAEYC Affiliate Groups across the nation to call public attention to the needs and rights of children and families

• **Insurance plans** for individuals and programs

• **Public affairs information** for knowledgeable advocacy efforts at all levels of government and through the media

• The **National Academy of Early Childhood Programs,** a voluntary accreditation system for high-quality programs for children

• The **National Institute for Early Childhood Professional Development,** providing resources and services to improve professional preparation and development of early childhood educators

• The **Information Service,** a centralized source of information sharing, distribution, and collaboration

For free information about membership, publications, or other NAEYC services...

• call NAEYC at 202-232-8777 or 1-800-424-2460,

• or write to the National Association for the Education of Young Children, 1509 16th Street, N.W., Washington, DC 20036-1426.